I0109786

Insights You Need from
**Harvard
Business
Review**

THE YEAR IN TECH,
2026

Insights You Need from Harvard Business Review

Business is changing. Will you adapt or be left behind?

Get up to speed and deepen your understanding of the topics that are shaping your company's future with the **Insights You Need from Harvard Business Review** series. Featuring HBR's smartest thinking on fast-moving issues—blockchain, cybersecurity, AI, and more—each book provides the foundational introduction and practical case studies your organization needs to compete today and collects the best research, interviews, and analysis to get it ready for tomorrow.

You can't afford to ignore how these issues will transform the landscape of business and society. The Insights You Need series will help you grasp these critical ideas—and prepare you and your company for the future.

Books in the series include:

Agile
Artificial Intelligence
Blockchain
Climate Change
Crypto
Customer Data and Privacy
Cybersecurity
ESG
The Future of Work
Generative AI
Hybrid Workplace
Monopolies and Tech Giants
Multigenerational Workplace
Racial Justice
Reskilling and Upskilling
Strategic Analytics
Supply Chain
Web3
The Year in Tech, 2024
The Year in Tech, 2025

Insights You Need from

Harvard Business Review

THE YEAR IN TECH, 2026

Harvard Business Review Press

Boston, Massachusetts

HBR Press Quantity Sales Discounts

Harvard Business Review Press titles are available at significant quantity discounts when purchased in bulk for leadership development programs, client gifts, or sales promotions. Opportunities to co-brand copies with your logo or messaging are also available. For details and discount information for both print and ebook formats, contact booksales@hbr.org or visit www.hbr.org/bulksales.

Copyright 2025 Harvard Business School Publishing Corporation

All rights reserved
Printed in the United States of America

10 9 8 7 6 5 4 3 2 1

No part of this publication may be reproduced, stored in or introduced into a retrieval system, or transmitted, in any form, or by any means (electronic, mechanical, photocopying, recording, or otherwise), without the prior permission of the publisher. Requests for permission should be directed to permissions@harvardbusiness.org, or mailed to Permissions, Harvard Business School Publishing, 60 Harvard Way, Boston, Massachusetts 02163.

The web addresses referenced in this book were live and correct at the time of the book's publication but may be subject to change.

Cataloging-in-Publication data is forthcoming.

ISBN: 979-8-89279-197-7
eISBN: 979-8-89279-198-4

The paper used in this publication meets the requirements of the American National Standard for Permanence of Paper for Publications and Documents in Libraries and Archives Z39.48-1992.

Contents

Contents

Section 2

Tech Stories with Big Impact

Section 3

Predicting and Building Your Company's Future

Introduction

THE MESSY MIDDLE OF DISRUPTIVE CHANGE

by Scott D. Anthony

In his 1620 classic *Novum Orangum*, Sir Francis Bacon noted three technologies—the printing press, the compass, and gunpowder—that "changed the appearance and state of the whole world." These inventions each created a line between *before* and *after*.

Additive manufacturing. Artificial intelligence. Autonomous vehicles. Cleantech. Cryptocurrencies. Drones. Lab-grown meat. Mixed reality. Robotics. Smart health. In the future we will likely look back and distinguish *before* and *after* each of these ongoing disruptions. Right now, however, things feel awfully messy.

That isn't unusual. My book *Epic Disruptions* explores 11 historical disruptions. One chapter focuses on the Model T car. Henry Ford's vision was to create a car for the "great multitude," one so affordable that, in Ford's words, "no man making a good salary will be unable to own."

Ford delivered. He followed the classic pattern of what we now call a disruptive innovation. He made an expensive, complicated product affordable and easy to use. He played a critical role in creating an industry that helped to create the modern world.

The Model T cost $850 when it debuted in 1908. That's roughly $30,000 in today's terms. By 1924 the development and refinement of the assembly line lowered that price to $260 or $5,000 in today's terms.

Lowering the cost of the automobile wasn't enough to usher in the automobile era. Success also required winning the battle for the soul of the streets of major cities. After all, cities were designed for pedestrians, horses, and mass transit. There were no traffic lights and no norms about how and where pedestrians should cross streets.

The sharp increase in automobile adoption spurred chaos and carnage.

Newspaper cartoons in the 1920s often showed the Grim Reaper driving cars. One in the *St. Louis Star* showed a man kneeling holding up a platter of children to a car with a humanoid maniacal grin. In 1922 the mayor of Baltimore dedicated a 25-foot wood and plaster obelisk as a monument for the 130 children who died in motor accidents that year.

A fierce public relations campaign broke out. Motorists coined a term for pedestrians who crossed roads in the wrong places or in the wrong ways. The word "jay" at the time meant an uneducated country dweller who was out of place in the city. Thus, the epithet *jaywalker*. Car enthusiasts enlisted Boy Scouts to distribute anti-jaywalking cards.

Pedestrians fought back. They sought to brand drivers who drove recklessly as *flivverboobs*. Flivver was slang for an automobile, typically one that was cheap or low quality. A boob, well, that's pretty timeless.

By 1924, the magistrate of the New York City Traffic Court ascribed somewhere between 70% and 90% of accidents to jaywalking. Today, if you type *flivverboob* into Microsoft Word, the distinctive red squiggle shows that the word is no longer in use. In fact, it largely disappeared after just a few years of use.

This was more than a marketing victory for Ford and other automotive manufacturers. It was a key step in the transformation of transportation.

More than a century after the triumph of the motorists, the world finds itself in the messy middle of a number of ongoing disruptions. *The Year in Tech, 2026* is an indispensable guide to cut through the noise and enable sound decision-making in the face of significant uncertainty. The collection starts with AI, of course, but expands to cover other critical stories in technology before concluding by providing guidance about how to predict and build your company's future.

History might not repeat, the saying goes, but it often rhymes. Four patterns that connect the historical disruptions in *Epic Disruptions* clearly appear in *The Year in Tech, 2026*.

1. Innovation is not the job of the few; it is the responsibility of the many. The lone inventor is a myth. Even innovation stories with a clear protagonist, such as Johannes Gutenberg's printing press, involve a wide cast of characters. Gutenberg had business partners, a financial backer (who sued him), customers, and so on. Yes, there must be a visionary who sees what others don't. But it requires *a lot* more on top of that. Innovation is a collectively individualistic act.

This theme comes across clearly in this collection. Disruptions such as AI and autonomous vehicles will only advance if there are parallel efforts to create system-level enablers and to develop the right enabling infrastructure. No lone actor is sufficient to solve such complex problems.

"It is the combination of labor, capital, and AI that will—if anything—generate the value that's being projected," José Parra-Moyano and Amit Joshi note in their contribution about the importance of data collectives. Technology is a critical piece of disruption, but it is only a piece. As Scott Zoldi and Jordan T. Levine describe in their overview of how FICO deployed blockchain to build trust, "getting this system up and running wasn't a technology problem, first and foremost. It was an organization and people problem."

2. Innovation is predictably unpredictable. There are clear patterns that cut across historical disruptions. McDonald's success, for example, mirrors Ford's efforts to develop an end-to-end system to create and support affordable automobiles. McDonald's wasn't the first hamburger restaurant. It wasn't the first company to franchise its model and menu. It wasn't the first to get to some kind of scale. But it *was* the first to put all the pieces together into its own end-to-end system.

While the broad patterns are predictable, every journey has its unique surprises and struggles. During the 1950s, for example, the McDonald's Corporation itself earned less than $200,000 in *aggregate* profits even as McDonald's franchises soared. Its assumption that financial success came from selling more hamburgers proved to be incorrect, or at least incomplete. Growth accelerated when it figured out the right formula to lock in profits through subleasing real estate to franchise owners. That McDonald's would tirelessly search for a way to scale profitably was predictable. The *specific* answer it discovered was unpredictable.

Whenever a broad disruptive trend develops, innovators seek a compelling strategy for success. By some count, there were more than 2,000 automobile manufacturers in the first two decades from 1900 to 1920. It's no surprise today that you have what seem like nearly constant shocking developments in hot and crowded spaces like AI, such as the launch of DeepSeek in early 2025 (detailed in Toby E. Stuart's article). That's one reason why asking "what if?" questions, like Amy Webb suggests in her article on "Living Intelligence," is indeed so critical. Try to imagine what seems unimaginable, because it might just become practical sooner than you think. When it comes to disruption, you need to expect the unexpected.

3. Innovation requires patient perseverance.
There is a lot of talk about the accelerating pace of change; how, for example, ChatGPT was the fastest innovation in history to get to one hundred million users. Yes, that specific use of AI was adopted quickly. However, ChatGPT launched in

what was arguably year 66 for AI, if you trace it back to a 1956 conference at Dartmouth College. What looks like rapid adoption in a short period is often the tail end of slow, steady background developments.

For example, also in 1956, Procter & Gamble commissioned a team to investigate the disposable diaper market. The company then created a product that bombed in its first test market because of low product quality, performed poorly in its second because it was overpriced, and still had only moderate success in its third. P&G persevered, and by 1970 had 92% of the disposable diaper market, which by then had exploded to be twice the size of the cloth diaper–servicing industry. Disruptive innovation requires being patient through twists, turns, false starts, and failures.

Autonomous vehicles follow this pattern. Tucker J. Marion, David Deeds, and John H. Friar eloquently trace the history of autonomous vehicles, showing how the same Ford Motor Company first showcased a version of the technology way back in 1925. Transformation, the authors note, comes not from a single technology but from a combination of them. A theme across several articles is the need to focus, to experiment, to try, to learn. In an engaging look at how 570 experts have divergent views of the future of work, Nicky Dries, Joost Luyckx, and Philip Rogiers note that "embracing uncertainty and competing scenarios is in fact essential to long-term strategic planning."

4. Disruption casts a shadow. Today, innovation is viewed as a positive good. It wasn't always. In 1548, Kind Edward VI (or his advisers; he was, after all, only 10) issued a "Proclamation Against Those That Doeth Innouate." Innovation wasn't a heroic act; it was an act of heresy against religious norms. Disruption by nature challenges the status quo, which might be good for the world but less good for those seeking to preserve that status quo. The introduction of disruption can be messy, as any pedestrian crying out "flivverboob!" might attest. Disruption changes the dynamics in organizations, industries, and society. That's good for some and bad for others. If you ignore the shadow that disruption casts, it can swallow you.

Today's tightly connected technologies cast their own shadow. Raphael Yahalom dissects what to take away from the CrowdStrike glitch, a seemingly straightforward content update that went awry and caused billions of dollars of damage. As exciting as AI can be, Christina Shim reminds us that it also has a heavy environmental footprint. Addressing these kinds of issues will be critical to maximize the positive impact of ongoing disruption—and mitigate inevitable backlashes.

. . .

About 1,600 years separate the oldest of Bacon's trinity of technologies (the compass) and the newest (the printing press). Today, it feels like we're on the brink of another before-and-after disruption every 1,600 minutes. As the stories are being written, keep these four historical lessons in mind. They will help you make sense of today's turbulence and turn today's ambiguity into tomorrow's opportunity.

Section 1

WHAT'S COMING NEXT WITH AI?

1

WHAT IS AGENTIC AI, AND HOW WILL IT CHANGE WORK?

by Mark Purdy

T he way humans interact and collaborate with AI is taking a dramatic leap forward with agentic AI. Think: AI-powered agents that can plan your next trip overseas and make all the travel arrangements; humanlike bots that act as virtual caregivers for the elderly; or AI-powered supply-chain specialists that can optimize inventories on the fly in response to fluctuations in real-time demand. These are just some of the possibilities opened up by the coming era of agentic AI.

While previous AI assistants were rules-based and had limited ability to act independently, agentic AI will be empowered to do more on our behalf. But what, exactly, *is* agentic AI? "You can define agentic AI with one word: proactiveness," said Enver Cetin, an AI expert at global experience engineering firm Ciklum, whom I interviewed. "It refers to AI systems and models that can act autonomously to achieve goals without the need for constant human guidance. The agentic AI system understands what the goal or vision of the user is and the context to the problem they are trying to solve."

To achieve this level of autonomous decision-making and action, agentic AI relies on a complex ensemble of different machine learning, natural language processing, and automation technologies. While agentic AI systems harness the creative abilities of generative AI models such as ChatGPT, they differ in several ways. First, they are focused on making decisions rather than on creating content. Second, they do not rely on human prompts but rather are set to optimize particular goals or objectives, such as maximizing sales, customer satisfaction scores, or efficiency in supply-chain processes. And third, unlike generative AI, they can also carry out complex sequences of activities, independently searching databases or triggering workflows to complete activities.

The Benefits of Working with Agentic AI

With their supercharged reasoning and execution capabilities, agentic AI systems promise to transform many aspects of human-machine collaboration, especially in areas of work that were previously insulated from AI-led automation, such as proactively managing complex IT systems to preempt outages, dynamically reconfiguring supply chains in response to geopolitical or weather disruptions, or engaging in realistic interactions with patients or customers to resolve issues. Three of the main benefits will be greater workforce specialization, greater informational trustworthiness, and enhanced innovation.

Greater specialization

The importance of workforce specialization—the "division of labor"—has been understood since Adam Smith's celebrated pin-factory visit in the opening paragraphs of *The Wealth of Nations*. Smith observed how one worker "draws out the wire, another straights [sic] it, a third cuts it; a fourth points it . . ." such that "the important business of making a pin is, in this manner, divided into about eighteen distinct operations." Specialization brings greater efficiency, learning by doing, and innovation—but can be difficult to implement as businesses run up against workforce shortages and mismatches between roles and available human skills. Because agentic models are explicitly designed to carry out very granular tasks, they enable much greater specialization of roles compared with previous broad-brush automation systems. What's more, multiple agentic roles can be created rapidly. In knowledge work, for example, agents can be created for information retrieval, analysis, workflow generation, and employee assistance—all working in tandem. Some AI agents will also work "behind the scenes," orchestrating the work of other agents, just as human managers do for their teams.

Innovation

With their enhanced judgment and powers of execution, agentic AI systems are ideal for experimentation and innovation. For example, ChemCrow, an AI-powered chemistry agent, has been used to plan and synthesize a new insect repellent as well as to create novel organic compounds. Multi-agent AI models can also scan and analyze vast research spaces—such as scientific articles and databases—in a fraction of the time it would take teams of human scientists and researchers. SciAgent—a multi-agent model developed by researchers at MIT—includes not only robot scientists to develop research plans, but a Critic Agent to review these and suggest improvements. Working together, the team of AI agents was able to identify a novel biomaterial combining silk and dandelion-based pigments that had better mechanical and optical properties than similar materials, while requiring less energy to boot.

Greater trustworthiness

The greater cognitive reasoning of agentic AI systems means that they are less likely to suffer from the so-called hallucinations (or invented information) common to generative AI systems. Agentic AI systems also have significantly greater ability to sift and differentiate information sources for quality and reliability, increasing the degree of trust in their decisions. For example, while customer information is often scattered in different formats across different parts of a business—emails, databases, spreadsheets, and the like—an agentic AI system can quickly discern that the most reliable and up-to-date information is likely to be in the firm's customer relationship management (CRM) systems. Agentic systems are also designed to quickly learn a company's human and brand values, ensuring that these are aligned with decisions and actions.

Potential Use Cases

While many applications of agentic AI are still experimental in nature or at a pilot stage, the broad contours of potential use cases are already starting to emerge across different industries and functions. Some examples include:

Customer service

In contrast to traditional automated customer bots that were preprogrammed with a limited range of responses and actions, agentic customer service agents can quickly grasp customer intents and emotions and take independent steps to resolve queries and problems. For example, an agentic customer service agent could predictively assess whether a customer delivery is going to be late, inform the customer of the delay, and proactively offer a discount to sweeten the disappointment. Ema, an AI startup based in California, offers agentic AI chatbots that can dynamically trawl thousands of different databases and apps to resolve customer queries and complaints, learning from each customer interaction and identifying recommended actions for human agents. Ema also audits its content for accuracy and compliance purposes, while also making recommendations to improve the customer knowledge base.

Manufacturing

From controlling the flow of production lines to customizing products to making suggestions for improved product design, agentic AI is likely to have multiple applications in smart manufacturing. Data from sensors attached to machines, components, and other physical assets in factories and transportation can be analyzed by an agentic AI system to predict wear-and-tear and production outages, avoiding unscheduled downtime and associated costs to manufacturers. German AI startup Juna.ai deploys AI agents to run virtual factories, with the aim of maximizing productivity and quality while reducing energy consumption and carbon emissions. It even offers agents tailored to specific goals, such as production agents and quality agents.

Sales support

For sales agents, the critical goal of finding and developing sales leads can often be swamped by a mass of emails, paperwork, and other mundane but necessary administrative tasks. Agentic AI systems could dramatically liberate sales teams from much of this time-consuming activity. CRM technology titan Salesforce, for example, recently introduced its Agent Force Service Development Rep to assist the work of human sales teams. Powered by large language models (LLMs), the agent can interpret customer messages, recommend follow-up actions, book meetings, answer questions, and generate responses that are attuned to the company's brand voice. Complementing these activities is the Agent Force Sales Coach, providing personalized feedback to human agents and opportunities for learning through virtual role-play sessions.

Health and social care

Their ability to adapt to different settings, interpret human emotions, and show empathy makes agentic AI systems ideal for nonroutine, soft-skills work in areas such as health care and caregiving. Hippocratic AI, an agentic AI health care company based in California, has created a phalanx of AI agents tailored to different areas of health care and social support. The team counts among its ranks Sarah, an AI agent who "radiates warmth and understanding" while providing help with assisted living. Sarah can ask patients about their day, organize menus and transport, and regularly remind patients to take their medication. Judy, another AI-powered agent, helps patients with preoperative procedures, for example by reminding patients about arrival time and locations, or advising on pre-op fasting or stopping medications.

The Challenges Ahead

Despite significant potential to transform human-machine collaboration and drive greater efficiency and business growth, agentic AI systems are still at a relatively early stage of development. Moreover, despite their greater powers of reasoning and execution, they do not remove traditional workforce management challenges; instead, they change them. Just as in traditional, human workforce settings, managers must still pay heed to issues of team composition and role selection, and they must set the right overall goals to ensure that agentic AI or hybrid teams can be successful. They must also carefully calibrate the conditions under which agentic AI systems can be trusted to make decisions and the circumstances in which human decision-makers need to intervene.

Imperatives for Success

To capitalize on the opportunities of agentic AI while mitigating the risks, managers should consider the following imperatives:

Set SMART goals

Just as the performance of human teams can be stymied by poorly defined or badly articulated goals, so too can agentic AI systems go off track if goals are not set clearly. In fact, goal setting becomes even more important for agentic AI, as the systems initially lack the contextual information—such as organizational and market context, company values, and so forth—that is often tacitly understood by human workers. Ciklum's Cetin underlines the importance of comprehensive goal setting: "For agentic AI to succeed, the models must have SMART (specific, measurable, achievable, relevant, time-bound) goals and subgoals and know how to measure them. They must have the right contextual information—why are these goals important to the company, how do they drive revenues, etc. Finally, as managers, we need to establish feedback loops to adjust the models as we learn more about their performance."

Pay attention to team selection

Compared to generative AI—which is largely based on prompting LLMs with singular questions—agentic AI is much more of a team endeavor, making use of multiple AI agents, all of whom have specific roles to play in achieving a greater goal, be it maximizing customer experience or innovating a lower-cost business process. Just as in human teams, problems of coordination, conflict, and resource management are likely to arise. Managers using agentic AI systems will need to pay careful attention to team selection, ensuring that they have the right combination of agentic roles carrying out the right tasks, in an efficient way. Furthermore, they will need to carefully consider how agentic teams interplay with human workers to achieve trust and efficiency in activities.

Scaffold the decision space

While agentic AI models are explicitly designed to evaluate choices and carry out complex sequences of actions, they are not foolproof and can still make mistakes, just as humans do. Learning science highlights the importance of "scaffolding" in learning, giving learners exposure to real-world practice with safeguards—supervision, well-defined limits, etc.—which are then progressively withdrawn as experience grows. Such scaffolding will be essential as agentic AI systems are applied to different tasks and business areas, with decision-makers constructing appropriate scaffolding for these models based on factors such as the criticality of the decision, the consequences of mistakes, the degree of confidence in the data used to train the models, the degree of human supervision, and the experience profile of the humans who work alongside these systems.

. . .

From the early days of mechanical automatons to more recent conversational bots, scientists and engineers have dreamed of a future where AI systems can work and act intelligently and independently. Recent advances in agentic AI bring that autonomous future a step closer to reality. The agentic AI prize could be great, with the promise of greater productivity, innovation, and insights for the human workforce. But so, too, are the risks: the potential for bias, mistakes, and inappropriate use. Early action by business and government leaders now will help set the right course for agentic AI development, so that its benefits can be achieved safely and fairly.

TAKEAWAYS

Agentic AI is revolutionizing the way humans interact and collaborate with AI. While previous AI assistants were rules-based and had limited ability to act independently, agentic AI will be proactive, acting autonomously to achieve goals without constant human guidance.

- ✓ **Greater specialization.** These systems enable more granular task specialization, improving efficiency and innovation.

- ✓ **Innovation.** Agentic AI is ideal for experimentation, rapidly analyzing vast research spaces and developing new solutions.

- ✓ **Trustworthiness.** With enhanced cognitive reasoning, agentic AI systems are less prone to errors than earlier forms of generative AI and can better differentiate information sources.

- ✓ **Potential use cases.** Applications include customer service, manufacturing, sales support, and health care.

✓ **Challenges.** Managers must set clearly defined situations and select the right teams to develop and train the models.

Adapted from HBR.org, December 12, 2024 (reprint #H08ISM).

2

USING BLOCKCHAIN TO BUILD CUSTOMER TRUST IN AI

by Scott Zoldi and Jordan T. Levine

I n a remarkably short period of time, organizations across industries have deployed artificial intelligence (AI) to produce decisions that affect people's daily lives. Since AI can be characterized as "a mirror that reflects our biases and moral flaws back to us," sometimes this practice results in unfortunate and even tragic mistakes. And bias is just one of a multitude of reasons why AI is considered a "black box" with a trust problem. Last year Pew Research found that 52% of Americans are more concerned than excited about AI in daily life, compared with just 10% who say they are more excited than concerned.[1]

Clearly, AI needs to prove itself as a trustworthy technology. To do this, companies that use AI must ensure the interpretability, auditability, and enforceability of decisions these analytic models make. *Interpretability* enables the technology to be understood. *Auditability* enables accountability. Finally, *enforceability* assuages doubt, leaving trust in its wake.

If organizations want to reap real business benefits from their investments in AI, customers need to trust it. Systemic social mistrust in AI can be dissolved only when questions about how this technology works—from customers, regulators, and other appropriate parties—can be answered. Using blockchain-based accountability provides an attainable, operational path to accountability and enforceability.

At FICO, we're using blockchain technology to build the trust of consumers and the financial industry at large in AI. Blockchain creates an immutable record of every aspect of AI model development and ensures that every action taken adheres to corporate requirements and standards for responsible AI. Rather than signaling mistrust in data scientists, a blockchain system for AI model management illustrates that trust is not a personal issue—there's a reason that important things in life have contracts. The blockchain doesn't serve to pinpoint blame; it's designed to keep everyone honest, efficient, safe, and on-standard. With proper governance and accountability structures in place, AI innovation has a safe and wide-open space to thrive.

This article presents a case study on how FICO came to adopt blockchain-based AI model development management, how it benefits the business, and how other organizations can adopt and gain from this approach.

When Blockchain Met AI

In 2021 the FICO data science team responsible for AI and analytic innovation began using blockchain for model development governance, a move that has since provided demonstrable value. This team provides core technology for FICO's software platforms, including fraud detection and solutions for credit card management, and is separate from the analytic organization that develops analytics for the FICO Score. It has found that this approach has not only sped our time to market with AI and analytic innovation but has also helped keep new models in production; blockchain has reduced support issues and model recalls by over 90%. It has done so by helping to automate the process of keeping tabs on the rapidly multiplying model development details.

The seeds of this approach were developed over more than a decade of work, as the team worked to document and manage the myriad incremental decisions that go into the complex process of developing a model: the model's variables, model design, algorithms, training, and test data utilized the model's raw latent features, ethics testing, and stability testing. This process also includes an enormous human element: the scientists who build different portions of the variable sets, participate in model creation, and perform model testing. Each tiny change can impact model performance, responsible use, and decision outcomes.

The initial solution the data science team came up with was to start using an analytic tracking document (ATD) to guide its development process. Originally contained in a pages-long Word document, this approach detailed every aspect of a model's requirements, development, and testing. The ATD informed a set of very specific requirements linked to FICO's AI model development standard. Once all elements of the build were negotiated, it became the document by which the team defined the entire model development process.

Using the ATD was a game changer, but handling hundreds of voluminous ATD model documents, and holding dozens of meetings to confirm each model's adherence to the standard, generated too much administrative overhead. So, in 2021, FICO put the entire ATD process onto a private blockchain, providing a much easier way to create an immutable trail of decision-making for every model. The blockchain eliminates any confusion about requirements, algorithms used, and success criteria to be met, as all are committed to the chain before development starts. It also permanently links to assets that demonstrate adherence to standards, exposes latent features, and determines if these introduce bias into the model, as well as identifying who worked on the latent features, which tests were done, the approving manager, and management sign-off.

Importantly, the blockchain produces not just a checklist of positive outcomes; it also includes mistakes, corrections, and improvements made along the way.

Why Blockchain Works

The ATD has come a long way from lengthy Word documents. FICO's blockchain-based approach abstracts each task into an easy-to-use interface that is integrated into data scientists' daily work. A maverick scientist who doesn't want to use this method, just can't—committing each development decision to the blockchain is simply the way the work gets done and a requirement for models to get released.

FICO has found the business value of blockchain's immutable record to be enormous. We achieve consistency in a large global data science organization; model development across hundreds of production analytic assets each year is uniform, minimizing confusion and waste.

Reducing waste matters, given the sky-high opportunity costs of lost innovation and the very tangible costs of AI development talent and related computing resources. It's an open secret in financial services that only a fraction of internally developed AI models is put into production because no one is quite sure what's in them or how they will perform. A 2019 McKinsey & Co. survey of the financial services sector found that only 25% to 36% of respondents had deployed AI in various use cases within their companies.[2] Anecdotally, we've seen those numbers improve, but across the industry, unused AI assets still translate into hundreds of millions of dollars of wasted effort.

Ultimately, FICO knows why blockchain works because of what *doesn't* happen. Models are not held back from production because of uncertainty about their risk or lack of artifacts demonstrating adherence to the company's Responsible AI standards. Scientists don't inadvertently tap production models for research projects or, worse, release data science experiments "into the wild." And that maverick data scientist? Time isn't wasted in rejecting work that goes rogue, intentionally or not; the blockchain keeps teams cohesive, on-standard, and meeting requirements, efficiently producing models that meet FICO's quality and safety standards. In addition to seeing model support issues drop to nearly zero, we achieve absolute adherence to, and enforceability of, AI model development standards even at high velocity.

All of this is the operational key to building trust in AI. It helps FICO produce output that 100% complies with our standards, backed with hard assets of proof of work. This means that consumers' experience of these tools is consistent with our own Responsible AI standards.

How FICO Made Blockchain Work for AI

Getting this system up and running wasn't a technology problem, first and foremost. It was an organization and people problem. Addressing that was followed by design and technological hurdles that had to be cleared, of course, but the first part was the hardest.

Here's what we learned through this process.

Standards first, tech second

Without an AI model development standard to adhere to, using blockchain to record every detail of model development is futile. Unfortunately, this first step can be the hardest part of the journey: To establish corporate standards around responsible AI, hard decisions will need to be made on what will and will not be done, including approvals of which algorithms can and can't be used, model interpretability, ethical AI testing methodologies, and meeting regulatory requirements. At FICO, this involved some evangelism around the goal of ensuring consistent analytic outcomes for all clients independent of individual data scientists' artistry and appointing a committee that would define the development standards and educate the entire team on associated methods.

User friendly is nonnegotiable

At FICO, getting the data scientists on board with the idea of using the system wasn't that hard. Most of them appreciated the structure it offers, automatic alignment of their work with AI model development standards, and formalized approaches to responsible AI, all of which protect them and their work products.

What *was* hard was developing the user interface (UI) between the data scientists and the blockchain. UI development was more than figuring out which fields and buttons the user would click and when; it had to help data scientists make the mental shift from individual-centric, linear waterfall development to a team mindset in which multiple developers and testers could do their work and validate others' in an efficient, automated way.

Ultimately, we invested significant time and resources to make it easy for scientists to use the system in a way that emphasizes intellectual engagement instead of cumbersome oversight, integrating a slick UI into the way work gets done.

To achieve that end state, organizations should prepare to go through a formal process with business requirements and product requirements documents (BRDs and PRDs). This allows software designers' thoughts and opinions to be aligned on how users will interact with the system and how the process will operate. It was important to ensure that everyone felt heard and that development didn't start until expectations on form, functionality, and operation aligned.

Most critically for adoption, friction was not an acceptable outcome, forcing software development creativity from the get-go. For example, we had to balance data scientists' not needing or wanting to know blockchain technology with mandated use of the tool based on it. Similarly, we needed instant reporting on the state of all model development and testing tasks without requiring data scientists to build reports.

Iterate on quick wins

Next, prepare to do proofs of concept of early designs to get a quick version of the system working, and start navigating use cases such as establishing requirements, development updates, testing updates, validation up-dates, rejection/approval, and how to reset the state of the requirements when a model is rejected. There should be a strong focus on how completeness is measured, since no model is released until all requirements are met by the developer, tester, and validator—how will that be parsed from the blockchain and presented to stakeholders?

Keep everything together, forever

No analytic application is ever truly done; it's constantly evolving, and processes (particularly for dependencies) cannot be forgotten. So, as a key technical point, it's important to think about the repositories that will hold large AI assets in alternate storage, with hashes, checksums, and other mechanisms that will confirm the asset referenced in the blockchain is appropriate and uncorrupted. Any alternate storage must be actively monitored and alerts issued if there are updates or migrations to other tech stacks within the organization.

Maintenance hits different

Finally, the overarching reality of a blockchain-based AI model development management system is that it is software—software with requirements for security and vulnerability management, maintenance, and upgrades. IT software teams handle these issues every day for enterprise applications, but with AI development applications, software developers need to cultivate new expertise or partner with other resources to get it.

· · ·

Trust can be elusive when working with AI. Understandably, these new powerful tools need to clear a high bar. But systemic mistrust in AI can only be dispelled when customers, regulators, and other appropriate parties are confident in how the technology works and that they can rely on specific models working the way they're supposed to. That's what this blockchain-based approach can provide: accountability, transparency, and enforceability. By keeping everyone honest, it gives users reason to trust these powerful new tools.

TAKEAWAYS

AI's increasing influence on daily life has led to growing concerns about its transparency, fairness, and reliability. Blockchain technology offers a solution by creating an immutable record of AI model development, ensuring accountability and adherence to ethical standards. FICO used this approach, and this article shares its learnings.

- ✓ Enhanced AI transparency. Blockchain tracks every stage of FICO's AI model development, reducing uncertainty and bias.

- ✓ Improved accountability. An immutable record prevents disputes and ensures adherence to responsible AI standards.

✓ **Simplified governance.** Automating model tracking streamlines compliance and reduces administrative burdens.

✓ **Usability must be prioritized.** Making these systems work is a people challenge as well as a technology challenge; a well-designed user interface fosters adoption among data scientists without adding friction.

NOTES

1. Alec Tyson and Emma Kikuchi, "Growing Public Concern about the Role of Artificial Intelligence in Daily Life," Pew Research Center, August 28, 2023, https://www.pewresearch.org /short-reads/2023/08/28/growing-public-concern-about-the-role -of-artificial-intelligence-in-daily-life/.

2. McKinsey & Company, "Global AI Survey: AI Proves Its Worth, but Few Scale Impact," November 22, 2019, https://www.mckinsey. com/featured-insights/artificial-intelligence/global-ai-survey-ai -proves-its-worth-but-few-scale-impact.

Adapted from HBR.org, January 20, 2025 (reprint #H08KST).

3

WHY ISN'T HEALTH CARE MORE PERSONALIZED?

by Robbie Hughes, J. Marc Overhage, and John Glaser

Now that electronic health records (EHRs) are ubiquitous, why does every other industry still leave health care in the dust when it comes to personalization? Nobody knows more about us than our health care providers, but they don't often leverage that electronic information to help their patients—or themselves. What will it take to make health care at least as personalized as our Amazon product recommendations?

EHRs and better communication across devices and systems have certainly helped. We can pay our physician visit co-pays, refill our prescriptions, and track our vital signs using an assortment of gadgets, and they can increasingly swap data with one another. We can check into our appointments the night before rather than arriving 15 minutes early to fill out yet another paper form. Our doctors can easily review what we discussed at our last visit, and the EHR can give them suggestions about possible diagnoses, tests to order, or the best treatments to try based on their exam findings and our description of our symptoms.

But there's still so far to go. While retailers, travel companies, banks, and brokerages use our personal information to finely tune the products and services they offer us (so finely that it verges on stalking), our health care providers still give us page after page of cookie-cutter, after-visit instructions that show little awareness of our often very specific health needs. Every patient for elective surgery may endure the hospital's standard list of presurgery tests, even if they got some of those identical tests just a week or two ago and the results are still valid and sitting right there in their EHR, or even if the surgeons don't really need every patient to have every test.

In 2021–2022, the team at Lumeon, a company that one of us (Robbie) headed, analyzed nearly 20,000 outpatient surgery cases in one health system and found that just under 70% of the patients didn't need one or more of the "standard" presurgical tests—either because the results were already on file with the health system or because the standard order sets were unnecessarily conservative. Additional analyses showed that a third of surgical delays and cancellations are due to labs not coming back on time or results not being reviewed. If that experience holds true across all providers (and research suggests that unnecessary tests are common), then we're delaying or canceling surgeries on a massive scale so we can wait for services that add nothing to the quality of our health or our care.

Further, those diagnosis and treatment protocols built into EHR software can't always accommodate variations in health status or account for patients' complicating conditions or their social situation (for instance, whether patients have transportation to appointments or access to the food they need to follow a special diet), even though their record may contain all that information somewhere. One study of cancer care pathways found that 65% of cancer patients were treated using one of the standard pathways and 35% were not.[1] (A pathway is a detailed, evidence-based treatment protocol that guides the delivery of care to patients with a particular type of cancer—from the initial diagnosis to end-of-life care. The pathway describes the specific medications, radiation regime, and surgical procedures to be used.) Moreover, the percent-age of patients treated using a pathway declined from 74% (2018) to 60% (2021). It's like taking a trip where you can't alter your route based on the weather, the need for fuel, or the desire to visit someone along the way. It's no wonder that clinicians don't take full advantage of such faulty "maps" and often don't trust them.

The Remedy

What's needed is smart process automation that employs artificial intelligence tools to find and use every shred of information that's applicable to a given scenario, combin-ing standardization and personalization to create the most effective and responsive care.

The need is dire—not just for patients but also for pro-viders. Health systems are under pressure. They face com-petition from new entrants with well-honed operations such as private equity-backed primary care groups and surgeons who own outpatient surgery centers. Patients who don't feel "known" by their health system may see no advantage in centralizing their care and will choose pro-viders on some other basis, whether it's price, location, or favorable Yelp reviews. Payers continue to move toward value-based reimbursement, which rewards providers who improve their patients' health rather than just supplying a certain volume of services. And every genomic mystery we unravel creates potential new opportunities—and new pressures—to personalize care.

What would a smarter process look like? Take the elective surgery example above. Knowing the procedure and the patient, AI-driven process automation could identify which tests and other types of care have already been done and which are needed, place the orders, confirm that tests have been scheduled and completed, and track the results. It could combine all those results to confirm that the patient can be cleared for surgery and then offer the patient a procedure time that's within the window where the results are still valid. If the patient chooses, the system could even put them on a wait list for an earlier slot and offer a schedule change in time for the patient to comply with pre-op instructions such as no food after midnight.

All those rote processes, informed by each patient's unique information and adapting whenever more information becomes available, can be done in the background, freeing clinicians and clerical staff for answering complex questions, hand-holding, and other functions that require the human touch.

One health system worked with Lumeon to implement the example above, and the results were impressive. It turned out that after using smart automation to analyze each patient's specific circumstances, 89% of patients could be adequately prepped for their procedures by some type of digital communication or, by exception, escalated to a short clarifying phone call and didn't require an in-person visit or the full battery of pre-op testing. The care team could spend its time on cases with a genuine need, resulting in happier patients, a happier care team, and better care.

Prior authorization—the bane of every provider's back office—is also ripe for redesign. Predictive models could identify diagnostic tests, procedures, or medications a patient is likely to need and automatically request the payer to approve them even before a provider has put in the orders. For example, if a patient with low back pain has worked through a full course of physical therapy and hasn't improved, an MRI of the lumbar spine might be a predictable next step. Having payer approval in hand in anticipation of that order would be a relief for both the clinician and the patient in pain.

The Building Blocks

The building blocks for these kinds of innovation are already in place, including:

A growing abundance of data

As noted earlier, the broad adoption of EHRs, the use of wearable devices, and the collection of data on social determinants of health, like access to food and transportation, have all led to a significant increase in the quantity and quality of data available to enable personalized care. For example, a process that plans a patient's post-surgery treatment can take into account that the patient lives alone and schedule a stay at a skilled nursing facility followed by home help.

This mass of data can also inform patients' choices. One unfortunate feature of today's health care is the lack of objective evidence for many common interventions, and even when evidence might exist, it may not have come to the attention of the office clinician. As a result, patients must rely on their physician's gut instinct, which might not be any better than their own in some cases.

Smart automation tools can marshal the available evidence that's most relevant to particular patients' situations and allow them to choose effective treatment options that also maximize their quality of life or improve the odds that they can adhere to the treatment path. And each patient's experience can be added to the evidence base for the treatment that individual chooses, enabling better choices for all patients.

Modular processes

Earlier paper and computerized versions of clinical-decision support systems and care pathways that described the best approach to treating a person with a specific disease used complex logic modules with dozens, if not hundreds, of interconnected branches and calculations. For example, the pathway for a disease might have a branch in logic for determining adjustments in care based on age and another branch might highlight treatment approaches that should be considered if a test result was highly abnormal. The combination of many branches and calculations were often hardwired together to form one very large pathway or care module that was often incomprehensible in aggregate and took a lot of work to maintain. This complexity was particularly common when it came to the care for people with cancer as well as those with several chronic diseases. These pathways could look like maps of the human brain that show every neuron.

Recent design innovations have broken these complex graphs into smaller, manageable modules that can be assembled in advance or dynamically as patient care progresses. This approach, known as modularization, acts like mass personalization, making the pathways more adaptable to specific contexts and significantly reducing the difficulty of maintaining and updating them.

For example, a care guideline might incorporate a new recommendation to schedule your first colonoscopy at age 45 or earlier if you have a bowel disease or a family history of colon cancer. Traditionally, new research influencing such guidelines could take over a decade to be reflected in general care recommendations. However, intelligent automation that employs modular processes can incorporate new risk factors and update recommendations much more swiftly and easily.

Deeper understanding of process design

Health care providers understand more than they ever have in the past about how to design processes to optimize care and influence patients' choices. These understandings include the use of "nudges" to influence a person's choice of options, approaches to redesigning care processes that distribute the work according to the talents and abilities of health care professionals and patients, and options for integrating process automation into the workflow of the care team.

The use of artificial intelligence

AI in general has the ability to learn from experience and guide processes based on that learning. It can analyze the many variables that influence process outcomes and suggest new process designs that personalize care based on those variables, extending process logic far beyond what had been previously considered practical.

For example, a predictive algorithm might show that a patient with well-controlled diabetes is nonetheless at risk of progressing to diabetes that is poorly managed due to a complex interaction of variables. It could indicate the degree of risk (high, medium, or low) and the factors that led to the risk score. This identification of factors would help clinicians and patients understand where medication and lifestyle changes are needed, and the risk score would determine the urgency of intervening.

Someday soon, we expect that when a human decision is required, generative AI will be able to summarize the data the decision-maker needs. It will be able to craft messages with the nuance needed to induce clinicians and patients to respond effectively when a process asks them to do something. For example, generative AI may summarize a patient's social circumstances and include links to social services that may be of assistance, even going so far as to coordinate them proactively as an independent, autonomous agent.

Finally, AI may decide which fork in the road to follow, within certain well-understood limits, leaving humans responsible for areas where evidence may be lacking or where human judgment remains the standard of care.

Getting Started

Where should providers begin the journey toward smart process automation and better personalization of our care? In addition to the usual planning process that surrounds such projects (allocating resources, establishing metrics, getting staff buy-in, and so on), we recommend two specific starting points:

Identify processes that are both high in volume and highly impactful when they fail

For instance, making an appointment is a frequent pain point for patients and can frustrate them to the point of abandoning their provider for one who has a less-annoying process. Processes that now can entail an hour or more on hold may be condensed, by using smart automation, to a few clicks through the patient portal that interpret the patient's intention, orchestrate it with the information in her EHR, and send her to the appropriate specialist nearest her home who has the earliest availability. The improvement in patient loyalty and retention may be hard to quantify, but we wouldn't want to be the last provider in a market to make this change.

At the organizational level, planning for patient discharges involves multiple decision points where minor variations can have a major impact on an expensive process. A lab test or MRI that's done half an hour behind schedule can end up keeping the patient in the hospital for an extra unnecessary night or vacating their bed so late that it causes a backup in the emergency department. Smart automation could generate a plan of care starting at the patient's admission and manage it on a minute-by-minute basis, integrating it with all the other patients' care plans to make sure both clinical and nonclinical activities are coordinated in the most efficient way.

Establish a reliable foundation of data gathered through consistent processes

The current delivery of care is littered with examples of clinicians repeating basic data-collection activities because they can't trust that they can rely on the existing data. Many AI models have been trained on data that's been collected over years of inconsistent processes, and they try to make predictions on data that we know is unreliable. Therefore, we must invest in understanding how we gather data and then use that understanding to eliminate inconsistency and build a new, clean dataset.

To be clear, we know that this will be a long journey and that the hype surrounding artificial intelligence is almost certain to lead to instances of keen disappointment and disillusionment as our industry realizes the path is much harder than we had been led to believe. Even the relatively limited transformation we have described above won't happen overnight, and it won't be particularly sexy. At best, it will get our health care to the same level of personalization that we enjoy today with online shopping or banking. But considering how dramatically that amount of transformation could improve everyone's health, we think that's more than enough.

TAKEAWAYS

Despite the widespread adoption of electronic health records (EHRs), health care remains far behind other industries in personalization. Smart process automation, leveraging AI and modular pathways that improve personalization and efficiency, could revolutionize health care.

- ✓ **EHRs aren't fully utilized.** Health care providers have vast patient data but fail to personalize care effectively.

- ✓ **Unnecessary tests and delays.** Standardized presurgery testing often disregards existing valid results, causing inefficiencies.

- ✓ **AI-driven automation can help.** AI can streamline test ordering, approvals, and patient scheduling, improving outcomes.

- ✓ **Modular processes enhance adaptability.** Breaking complex care pathways into smaller, flexible modules allows better personalization.

✓ **Data consistency is crucial.** Reliable data collection is necessary to improve AI-driven health care solutions.

✓ **Getting started.** Providers should focus on high-impact, high-volume processes like appointment scheduling and discharge planning.

NOTES

1. Y. Liu, S. Mullangi, D. Debono, et al., "Association Between Oncology Clinical Pathway Utilization and Toxicity and Cost Outcomes in Patients with Metastatic Solid Tumors," *JCO Oncology Practice* 2023, no. 19 (September 2023): 731–740, https://pubmed.ncbi.nlm.nih.gov/37384847/.

Adapted from HBR.org, November 21, 2024 (reprint #H08HDS).

4

WHY "LIVING INTELLIGENCE" IS THE NEXT BIG THING

by Amy Webb

Recently I was sitting across the table from the executive leadership team of a global health care services company, and I could tell by their body language that something was off. They'd invited me in to consult on their AI strategy, but they seemed defensive. The chief information officer, a sharp guy who'd clearly done his homework on emerging tech, launched into a detailed explanation of their new large language model. It was impressive, no doubt. This model automated their insanely complex data entry process—think mountains of handwritten patient forms and a chaotic mix of digital files—and consolidated everything into a single, coherent record. They'd spent well over a year developing and testing it and were understandably proud of their accomplishment. But as he talked about the rollout, it was obvious to me that they were already lagging behind.

"You've built an incredible foundation," I said, "but this is just the starting line." The energy in the room shifted. This wasn't the reaction they were expecting. Here was a company that had invested heavily in AI, built a sophisticated system, and deployed a successful pilot. Like so many other executive leadership teams who've spent the past year building and implementing AI tools, they thought they were *done*. In reality, their transformation had only begun. AI is merely one facet of a sweeping technological change underway, and companies that fail to recognize the importance of other converging technologies risk being left behind.

The Era of Living Intelligence

During my meeting with the company's executive team, I acknowledged that like so many leaders, the recent hyperfocus on AI, though late, was the right move. However,

LLMs were just a starting point. With new developments happening at a breakneck speed, the company would need to build a new muscle for continuous transformation. That's because AI is just one of three groundbreaking technologies shifting the business landscape. The other two—advanced sensors and biotechnology—are less visible, though no less important, and have been quietly advancing. Soon, the convergence of these three technologies is going to underpin a new reality that will shape the future decisions of every leader across industries.

I call this new reality "living intelligence": systems that can sense, learn, adapt, and evolve, made possible through artificial intelligence, advanced sensors, and biotechnology. Living intelligence will drive an exponential cycle of innovation, disrupting industries and creating entirely new markets. Leaders who focus solely on AI without understanding its intersections with these two other technologies risk missing a wave of disruption already forming.

The Everything Engine Needs Your Data

If AI is the everything engine, that engine needs data. Most likely, much of that data will come from advanced sensors and a network of interconnected devices that communicates and exchanges data to facilitate and fuel the advancement of AI. This function is why sensors are the next general-purpose technology—a fact that many leaders are currently missing.

Most people don't realize that sensors are already everywhere and are being put to use in multiple industries. It's an understandable oversight; we often use technology without thinking about it. But once you start to look for them, they're everywhere. For example, an iPhone comes embedded with a dozen sensors, ranging from proximity sensors to detect nearby objects to face ID sensors to authenticate a user. All of them mine and refine your data, all day long. Xylem, a water technology company, developed a new type of water meter that leverages advanced sensors and AI to manage the challenges of water distribution in densely populated settings. The meters continuously measure water flow and provide granular data on consumption patterns; they can also identify anomalies in water flow, like drops in pressure or irregular usage patterns, that typically result from a leak. Meanwhile, a new class of biological sensors can be worn and ingested. Their purpose: to send and receive data in real time in order to diagnose and monitor disease, detect pathogens, and enable faster recovery. One such biosensor includes a subclass of tiny machines, called nanobots, that can monitor patient health in real time after being injected into the bloodstream. Acting as internal surveillance systems, nanobots can detect changes in environmental stimuli and conditions, allowing for continuous health monitoring and early diagnosis of potential health issues.

As more sensors surround us, they will capture and transmit not just more data, but more types of data. While organizations are busy creating and using LLMs, they will soon need to build LAMs: large action models. If LLMs predict what to say next, LAMs predict what should be done next, breaking down complex tasks into smaller pieces. Unlike LLMs that primarily generate content, LAMs are optimized for task execution, enabling them to make real-time decisions based on specific commands, and will be enormously helpful in organizations of every size and scope. The earliest examples of LAMs are Anthropic's Claude and ACT-1 from Adept.ai. Both are designed to directly interact with code and digital tools and perform actions within software applications like a web browser. LAMs are like LLMs, but with more data and multimodal requirements. They will use the behavioral data we generate when we use our phones or operate our vehicles, along with a constellation of sensors everywhere, all around us, collecting multiple streams of data at once from wearables, extended reality devices, the internet of things, the home of things, smart cars, smart offices, and smart apartments. As LAMs become more embedded in our environments, they will operate seamlessly, often without users' direct engagement.

What so many organizations are failing to imagine is how LAMs will evolve to personal large action models, or PLAMs, and will eventually interact with different systems, learn from large datasets, and adapt to changing business needs. PLAMs will have the capacity to improve our digital, virtual, and physical experiences by streamlining decision-making, managing tasks, negotiating deals, and anticipating our needs based on behavioral data. They won't need conscious input. These autonomous agents will be able to personalize recommendations, optimize purchases, and communicate with other trusted agents, allowing seamless transactions—all while maintaining a user's privacy and preferences, since PLAMs, by definition, have access to all of the user data on personal devices.

In the near future, companies like Apple or Google will be motivated to embed even more smart sensors in devices to continuously collect and analyze personal data, such as health metrics, location data, and information about daily habits. All this data will be used to create highly individualized profiles that link to personal language and action models, tailored specifically to each user's needs and preferences. While people will have PLAMs, corporations will likewise have one or more corporate large action models (CLAMs), and digital-forward governments will have government large action models (GLAMs).

Artificial Intelligence Meets Organoid Intelligence

Living intelligence's third general-purpose technology is bioengineering, which involves using engineering techniques to build biological systems and products, such as designer microbes, which can be engineered specific tasks. Right now, this is the easiest to dismiss, but in the longer term it could prove to be the most important general purpose technology. Paired with AI, bioengineering can create "generative biology" (genBio), which uses data, computation, and AI to predict or create new biological insights—generating new biological components, such as proteins, genes, or even entire organisms, by simulating and predicting how biological elements behave and interact.

We can already see the potential of this technology. Companies like Ginkgo Bioworks are using genBio to design and create custom enzymes that can be applied in industrial processes. For example, generative algorithms help engineer enzymes that break down complex molecules, such as plastics or other pollutants. Google DeepMind created AlphaProteo, which designs completely new proteins with specific new properties that could have applications in biomaterials and drug development. Another project from DeepMind, a tool called GNoME (Graph Networks for Materials Exploration) has already predicted the stability of millions of new inorganic materials. Imagine a building made of materials that can autonomously self-regulate temperature, light, and ventilation—without a computer (or a human) in the loop.

Farther out, living intelligence could lead to living machines. Organoid intelligence (OI) made its debut as a new field of science in 2024. OI uses lab-grown tissues, such as brain cells and stem cells, to create biological computers that mimic the structure and function of the human brain. An organoid is more or less a tiny replica of tissue that functions like an organ of the body. In 2021, researchers at Cortical Labs in Melbourne, Australia, made a miniature organoid brain that worked like a computer. They called it DishBrain, attached it to electrodes, and taught it how to play the 1980s video game Pong. DishBrain is made of about 1 million live human and mouse brain cells grown on a microelectric array that can receive electrical signals. The signals tell the neurons where the Pong ball is located, and the cells respond. The more the system plays, the more it improves. Cortical Labs is now developing a new kind of software, a biological intelligence operating system, which would allow anyone with basic coding skills to program their own DishBrains.

How to Position Your Organization to Succeed

Although living intelligence may seem like a futuristic idea, forward-thinking CEOs and business leaders cannot afford to wait. We're already seeing the signs of convergence in living intelligence technologies across several leading-edge industries. Early adoption is happening most intensively in industries like pharmaceuticals, medical products, health care, space, construction and engineering, consumer packaged goods, and agriculture. But applications are coming to other industries soon, creating novel white spaces of opportunity in industries like financial services. As additional industries jump on board, innovation will disperse much more broadly, fueling additional flywheel effects.

We're going to see a compounding advancement as each technology improves. Here are five recommendations for how to act with diligence and urgency:

1. **Demystify living intelligence for the entire organization.** Senior leaders should familiarize themselves with living

intelligence—how AI, advanced sensor data, and bioengineering intersect.

2. **Develop pragmatic scenarios for disruption and new value generation.** Leaders should develop near- and long-term scenarios for using and scaling living intelligence technologies, processes, and products. Companies must use strategic foresight to understand how the evolving living intelligence ecosystem could have an impact on their existing products and processes.

3. **Identify two or three high-impact use cases—and just get started.** Leaders should pinpoint specific use cases where living intelligence can make the most significant impact. By choosing pilots with the greatest potential for scalability, leaders can accelerate the adoption of living intelligence and begin integrating these technologies into everyday workflows.

4. **Commit to developing the necessary roles, skills, and capabilities.** Living intelligence demands a mindset shift across the organization. Prioritize education and experimentation initiatives to prepare employees to work effectively alongside these technologies and develop new job

categories and descriptions for your workforce of the future.

5. **Monitor regulatory shifts and be prepared for policy uncertainty.** Living intelligence is bound to spark innovations and will demand unprecedented agility from companies, especially given the current patchwork regulatory approach. Leaders must empower their organizations to experiment with new products and processes and ensure that they shape their own futures rather than being compelled to adapt to external innovations or react to regulatory shifts.

Perhaps the most valuable recommendation I can offer is to simply ask, "What if?" At my next meeting with the health care company, I asked the executive leadership team to consider scenarios for how their business might transform in the coming decade as living intelligence matures. What if there was a "health assurance" subscription package that includes wearable sensors, AI-powered diagnostics, and personalized medication delivery? What if traditional providers were bypassed entirely, and startups used AI and sensor data to offer personalized health solutions directly to consumers? What if today's bathroom is tomorrow's diagnostic lab? What if real-time data led to real-time reporting on patient outcomes? Would there be a shift to outcome-based pricing? Meaning, would providers get paid based on the effectiveness of their treatments? All of these represent a significant shift in value generation.

Resist the temptation to fixate on AI as it exists today, I told the team. Take a more holistic view of the change already underway, and prepare your organization for the era of living intelligence.

TAKEAWAYS

Artificial intelligence is just one part of a larger technological shift. The convergence of AI, advanced sensors, and biotechnology is creating "living intelligence"—systems that sense, learn, adapt, and evolve. Organizations that focus only on AI risk falling behind as these two other transformative technologies redefine industries.

✓ **Sensors as data engines.** Advanced sensors will fuel AI with real-time data, leading to new decision-making models.

✓ **From large language models to large action models.** AI will evolve from generating text to executing real-world tasks.

✓ **Bioengineering meets AI.** Advances in biotechnology will create "generative biology" and even biological computers.

✓ **Acting now to prepare for disruption.** Leaders must educate their organizations, identify use cases, and build capabilities for this transformation.

Adapted from HBR.org, January 6, 2025 (reprint #H08JDL).

Section 2

TECH STORIES WITH BIG IMPACT

5

WHAT THE CROWDSTRIKE GLITCH CAN TEACH US ABOUT CYBER RISK

by Raphael Yahalom

O n July 19, 2024, a single content update from Crowd-Strike, a cybersecurity software company, caused more than 8.5 million systems to crash, disrupting operations for days across thousands of organizations worldwide, including hundreds of *Fortune* 1000 companies. The CrowdStrike "glitch," as it became known, resulted in losses estimated to be more than $5 billion.[1] The CrowdStrike incident is estimated to have cost insurers around $1.5 billion in payouts, under business interruption, cyber, and system failure coverages. It represents one of the biggest examples of the adverse impact of aggregated cyber risk accumulation. In October 2024, Delta, one of the many affected businesses in the incident, filed a lawsuit against CrowdStrike claiming that the outage was "catastrophic."[2] The airline claimed it was the result of CrowdStrike's "forced untested updates to its customers" and led to disruption of 7,000 flights and 1.3 million customers over five days. The airline claimed a loss of more than $500 million.

CrowdStrike in response, while admitting the root cause was a fault in its software update, claimed that "Delta's claims are based on disproven misinformation, demonstrate a lack of understanding of how modern cybersecurity works, and reflect a desperate attempt to shift blame for its slow recovery away from its failure to modernize its antiquated IT infrastructure."[3]

In this article we examine what managers and executives can learn from this incident. We discuss the outage's aftermath on the global state of cyber risk management, and we detail what organizations should be doing differently to prevent similar disruptions.

Companies Aren't Prepared

The overall number of cyber incidents, and the magnitude of their impact, continue to grow and worsen, despite advances in cybersecurity solutions and increased cybersecurity spending by organizations.

According to IBM's "2024 Cost of Data Breach Report," the average cost of a data breach in 2024 was $4.88 million, an increase of 10%.[4] Verizon's 2024 annual "Data Breach Report" analyzed 30,458 cybersecurity incidents, of which 10,626 were confirmed data breaches—a record high.[5]

A recent cyber risk market survey conducted by Milliman identified important gaps with significant market implications:[6]

- **A highly fragmented cybersecurity market:** Multiple solution directions with limited capabilities to unify these for credible comprehensive overall cyber risk management.

- **Cybersecurity decisions are based on disjointed data points:** A variety of cyber scores, local assessments, and questionnaires with insufficient end-to-end cyber risk perspectives.

- **Ineffective assessments of cyber risk concentration:** Limited capabilities to capture cyber dependencies necessary for identifying systemic cyber risk and risk aggregation.

- **A soft cyber insurance market:** Cyber underwriting methods are hard to reconcile due to insufficient historical data, quickly evolving threats, and too much subjectivity in making assessments.

- **Limited cyber risk transparency across organizations:** Supply chain cyber risk management is a big and growing challenge, and insufficient visibility is impacting cyber risk decisions.

- **New cyber risk challenges introduced by new emerging technologies:** AI, quantum computing, cloud computing, and other innovations lead to evolving regulatory requirements and increased cyber risk uncertainty.

The CrowdStrike incident is an important demonstration of all of these market gaps. Below, we use the CrowdStrike event to present four fundamental questions that should be part of your regular cyber risk reviews. Not only were these questions not adequately addressed by CrowdStrike and other impacted parties, but the industry lacks the appropriate methods to properly address such questions.

Four Open Questions About Cyber Risk

1. What is the level of risk of a CrowdStrike content update? (Does it reduce or increase overall risk?)

CrowdStrike's Falcon software is one of the leading cybersecurity solutions in the market. Content updates are CrowdStrike's mechanism for rapidly upgrading all its endpoint deployments to reflect emerging patterns of new cyber threats. They are designed to improve overall protection.

Due to the rapid emergence of new cyber threats, CrowdStrike may issue multiple such content updates per day. Since the market introduction of the Falcon solution in June 2013 CrowdStrike has issued many thousands of content updates to its global customers, with almost no reported problems.

But the risk associated with a content update is never zero. There is always some likelihood that software bugs will be exposed and cause disruption or other adverse effects. Therefore, the risk associated with implementing a content update needs to be assessed relative to the risk(s) that are eliminated by the improved protections embedded in the update. Effective approaches for performing such systematic and quantifiable analysis are currently not available.

In its lawsuit filing against CrowdStrike, when referring to the content update, Delta made claims such as:

- "By installing its exploit in Delta systems without Delta's permission or knowledge, CrowdStrike obstructed, interrupted, and interfered with Delta's use of its computer programs and computer networks."

- And, that as a result, "Delta suffered over $500 million in out-of-pocket losses from the Faulty Update, in addition to reputational harm and future revenue loss."

No reference was made to the fact that thousands of such "exploits" (content changes) have been installed by CrowdStrike in Delta systems successfully since it became a customer in 2022. No reference was made to the overall business value that these "exploits" provided Delta over that period in the form of enhanced protection against potential cyberattacks.

2. How should the risk of a CrowdStrike update be mitigated in an optimal manner? (Should it be applied immediately or delayed?)

The answer depends on the nature of the update and the nature of the target system (and its potential business impact). It requires a nuanced, systematic, and quantifiable balancing between the risk of adverse downstream business consequences due to a possible faulty update to that system (risk reduced as the delay is increased) and the business risk and escalation opportunities in case this system undergoes a cyberattack without the added protection (risk grows as the delay is increased).

In its October 2024 lawsuit, Delta claimed:

> *When CrowdStrike deployed the Faulty Update, CrowdStrike even forced its updates onto customers who had automatic updates disabled, such as Delta. Delta had not enabled the automatic update setting, because Delta wanted to maintain the proper type of change management controls over how updates could affect its computer systems and networks.*

Indeed, CrowdStrike treated its content updates as zero-risk events. Following the 2024 incident, CrowdStrike realized its risk management mistake and changed its deployment process for content updates to reflect the fact that they are associated with a level of risk that should be properly managed. Such improved transparency and customer control is clearly required. But the industry has struggled to determine what additional information should be provided and how customers can use it to make appropriate business-risk-aligned decisions.

3. How to ensure an optimal level of business resiliency when a content update is faulty.

This question requires a subtle systematic risk management analysis that captures all the various cyber dependencies involved. The industry is missing effective methods for systematic reasoning, and much of the current discussion is vague and ambiguous. For example, in its lawsuit Delta claims that CrowdStrike knew that its actions could harm Delta, its computers, its computer networks, and computer programs. But even the most high-quality development processes, testing, and certification may occasionally result in some form of a faulty output.

Delta provided no specific details in its lawsuit about its infrastructure's resiliency setup beyond some very general statements such as, "As part of its IT-planning and infrastructure, Delta has invested billions of dollars in licensing and building some of the best technology solutions in the airline industry," and "Delta is known for its customer service, reliability, and operational efficiency."

On the other hand, CrowdStrike and Microsoft have made general, controversial claims suggesting that Delta may have had an inferior resiliency setup compared to other leading airlines, resulting in a longer time to recover following the incident: "Our preliminary review suggests that Delta, unlike its competitors, apparently has not modernized its IT infrastructure, either for the benefit of its customers or for its pilots and flight attendants," according to CrowdStrike's lawsuit.

No specific details are provided, but such cyber resiliency analysis and comparison needs to be performed in a systematic and rigorous manner to ensure credible conclusions and apples-to-apples comparisons. Furthermore, both Microsoft and CrowdStrike made some unusual resiliency-related statements, indicating that in response to the incident their respective CEOs tried to contact Delta's CEO to offer recovery assistance.

CrowdStrike claimed that CEO George Kurtz reached out to Delta CEO Ed Bastian to "offer onsite assistance but received no response." Similarly, Microsoft claimed that it "immediately offered to assist Delta at no charge and that its CEO Satya Nadella emailed Bastian, but never got a reply."

While commendable, it is not at all clear how valuable CEO-level interactions are after automatic resiliency and recovery processes should have been triggered (or indeed whether Delta's CEO even had access to his email system at that point or if it was down due to CrowdStrike's faulty update).

4. How can we ensure accountability for losses?

CrowdStrike quickly took responsibility for its faulty update and apologized to the market. With respect to its financial liability in particular disputes such as the one with Delta, CrowdStrike indicated that "its contractual liability is capped in the single-digit millions," implying that it is not liable for most of the financial losses that are due to ineffective cyber-resilience measures by its customers.

While such specific disputes will be resolved in the pending lawsuits, we note that cyber information flow boundaries and accountability implications are generally ill defined and often ambiguous. Furthermore, there are cyber dependencies on multiple third parties that introduce additional accountability questions.

Consider, for example, Microsoft's role in the dispute between Delta and CrowdStrike. What is the precise relationship between Microsoft's commitment to test and certify all Windows kernel-access software and Crowd-Strike's faulty update?

Delta indicated that it "has reason to believe Microsoft has failed to comply with contractual requirements and otherwise acted in a grossly negligent, indeed willful, manner in connection with the Faulty Update." Microsoft suggested that Delta's ineffective cyber recovery may have been due to its reliance in various ways on infrastructure providers such as IBM and Amazon. Clearly, deriving cyber risk accountability conclusions in a systematic and credible manner among respective parties requires effective analysis frameworks that don't yet exist.

The Road Ahead: Explainable Cyber Risk Management

Although the CrowdStrike incident was not an actual cyberattack, there are many common characteristics and important lessons for all organizations related to such digital risk scenarios—whether accidental or deliberate.

Organizations should develop adequate capabilities to perform the following:

- Determine the "what-if" potential downstream business impact (direct and escalated) of a cyber event at any supply-chain partner (cyber compromises or errors). Delta and many other organizations may not have considered a priori important potential risk scenarios such as faulty CrowdStrike updates and their potential implications.

- Establish appropriate cyber resiliency business objectives and processes for any impactful cyber event at a supply-chain partner. The wide variations in recovery times and business losses in the CrowdStrike incident imply that multiple organizations did not have adequate cyber resiliency measures in place for such scenarios.

- Assess continuously the likelihood levels and interdependence of cyber events (internal and external) and make timely adjustments when required. CrowdStrike allegedly did not properly assess the likelihood of potential faults in its content update processes and consequently could not take appropriate corrective actions in time.

- Ensure effective communication (internally and externally) to provide adequate transparency as a basis for appropriate cyber risk management decisions. CrowdStrike's after-the-fact move to enable customers' control over when to apply content updates is a step in the right direction. But additional information on the digital risk attributes of each update needs to be shared as well to enable customers to make optimal decisions in each case.

- Specify well-defined accountability boundaries between relevant parties related to potential cyber risk scenarios and their business implications. The CrowdStrike incident highlights significant ambiguities and inconsistencies among counterparties regarding respective cyber risk-related commitments and expectations.

Most current cyber solutions in organizations focus on specific local targets but fall short of providing end-to-end cyber risk insights in a systematic, credible, and justifiable manner. A new paradigm of explainable cyber risk management is required. It must enable end-to-end scenario-based cyber risk analysis insights and maps between cyber events and business outcomes. For example, with respect to incidents such as CrowdStrike, a new approach would enable systematically assessing the business outcome scenarios of potentially faulty updates and balancing mitigation processes and recovery processes accordingly in a systematic and cyber-risk optimized manner.

Overall, we need better methods to develop higher levels of trust between users and service providers. Occasional unintentional technology failures are inevitable. Malicious cyberattacks will continue to grow in scale, scope, and impact with the increased global reliance on emerging digital technologies. Much more effective cyber risk management approaches are therefore urgently needed—and they must be transparent, structured, justifiable, and agile.

TAKEAWAYS

Data breaches and systemic failures are increasing, with major financial and operational consequences. The 2024 CrowdStrike glitch, which caused over 8.5 million system crashes and billions of dollars in losses, highlights the growing challenges in cyber risk management. To mitigate risks, businesses must adopt more structured and transparent cyber risk strategies.

✓ **Fragmented risk management.** Organizations lack unified approaches to assess and mitigate cyber risk effectively.

✓ **Software updates pose risks.** Even trusted cybersecurity updates can introduce failures, requiring better testing and deployment controls.

✓ **Resilience varies.** Companies with stronger IT infrastructure recover faster, while others suffer prolonged outages.

✓ **Accountability is unclear.** Cyber risk responsibilities between vendors and clients remain legally and operationally ambiguous.

✓ **Cyber risk management should be explainable.** Organizations must adopt scenario-based risk analysis to anticipate and mitigate future cyber failures.

NOTES

1. Brian Fung, "We Finally Know What Caused the Global Tech Outage—and How Much It Cost," CNN.com, July 24, 2024, https://www.cnn.com/2024/07/24/tech/crowdstrike-outage-cost -cause/index.html.

2. David Shepardson, "CrowdStrike, Delta Sue Each Other over Flight Disruptions," Reuters, October 28, 2024, https://www

.reuters.com/legal/crowdstrike-delta-sue-each-other-over-flight
-disruptions-2024-10-28/.

3. Ashley Belanger, "TSA Silent on CrowdStrike's Claim Delta
Skipped Required Security Update," ArsTechnica, October 29,
2024, https://arstechnica.com/tech-policy/2024/10/crowdstrike
-accuses-delta-of-blaming-its-own-it-failures-on-global-outage/.

4. "Cost of a Data Breach Report 2024," IBM.com, https://www
.ibm.com/reports/data-breach.

5. Verizon Business, "2024 Data Breach Investigations Report,"
https://www.verizon.com/business/resources/Te3/reports/2024
-dbir-data-breach-investigations-report.pdf.

6. Kimberly Guerriero, Téa Bourdeau, and Sam Raphael, "Is Cyber
Insurance Still Relevant for the Captive Market?" white paper,
Milliman, October 10, 2023, https://www.milliman.com/en
/insight/is-cyber-insurance-still-relevant-for-captive-market.

Adapted from "What the 2024 CrowdStrike Glitch Can Teach Us About Cyber Risk," on HBR.org, January 10, 2025 (reprint #H08KUZ).

6

DATA COOPERATIVES ARE THE NEXT FRONTIER OF LABOR RELATIONS

by José Parra-Moyano and Amit Joshi

The impact of AI, and generative AI in particular, is being felt across industries. But while executives are excited about this technology's potential, white-collar workers are often wary about what it may mean for them, their jobs, and their futures. These differing perceptions are creating new tensions and presenting new challenges for both groups.

Already, workers have taken action to exert their influence on the agenda that will determine what organizations will (or will not) do with AI. Most notably, there's the 148-day-long strike organized in 2023 by the Writers Guild of America (WGA), a union that represents 11,500 screenwriters. The strike ground the entertainment industry to a halt for months before finally ending with an agreement that AI can't write or rewrite literary material, that AI-generated material will not be considered source material (meaning that AI-generated material can't be used to undermine a writer's credit or separated rights), that the exploitation of writers' material to train AI is prohibited, and that writers can choose to use AI when performing writing services, but the company can't require the writer to use AI software when performing writing services.

This outcome was heralded as a win for the WGA, but it also illustrates the difficulties of these kinds of negotiations. First, the agreement expires in three years, meaning that the writers will be forced to renegotiate very soon. Second, it is not clear how the agreement will be enforced, since there is no guaranteed way to check whether or not data has been ingested by an LLM. Third, the agreement says nothing about outsiders entering the industry. OpenAI has started a campaign to promote Sora—its AI-based video generation tool—among filmmakers and studios in Hollywood. In principle, nothing prevents studios and filmmakers from starting to generate scripts and videos with OpenAI's tool, something that would significantly diminish not only the influence and power of writers, but of actors too.

While the WGA strike is the biggest example of employee action, it's not the only one. Employers need to start preparing for the possibility that anxiety over AI will spur white-collar unionization efforts and collective action. The AI Bill Project launched by the Trades Union Congress—a federation of trade unions representing blue- and white-collar unionized workers in England and Wales—shows evidence of how unions are rapidly evolving to increase the say of workers in how technology is used at work.[1]

All of the problems above are rooted—directly or indirectly—in access to high-quality, contextual data. Data is the input that is needed for machine learning algorithms to perform, and AI is made of such algorithms. Hence, those having access to high-quality data can train high-quality AI. Currently, the WGA does not govern the generation and use of data created by a workforce, and the latest data protection regulations like the EU AI Act focus on preventing employee monitoring but not on how content generated by the employees can be used to train models. Consequently, there is tremendous scope for conflict. And unless workers and organizations can address this data issue in a meaningful, lasting way, conflict will continue to be litigated through standoffs and piecemeal negotiations.

Data cooperatives offer one meaningful path forward. They are an organizational model that enables individuals to pool their data with the purpose of gaining bargaining power with the companies analyzing their data. Cooperatives like Swash, datum, MIDATA, Gener8, SAOS, GISC, and the Data Workers' Union provide avenues for individuals to monetize and manage their data, transforming its role—and theirs—in the digital economy. These cooperatives emphasize individual control, ethical use, and fair treatment and allow users to retain ownership and agency over their digital footprint. Furthermore, they offer in many cases the for-profit monetization of the data from the cooperatives' members, enabling third parties to get insights from that data (in a responsible and privacy-preserving way). Thus, data cooperatives can satisfy a demand for data-based insights or AI training. Simultaneously, they provide organizations with regularly updated, high-quality data that is extremely relevant to their context. This means that members have control over their data and they can give permission for specific companies to use it responsibly.

Data as a New Factor of Production

The impact of technology on employees and their employers is usually analyzed as a zero-sum game between both parties, in which automation increases profits for employers while it reduces jobs for employees.[2] However, AI's dependency on fresh data upends this view for three reasons:

- Generative AI's content-producing abilities can affect roles such as advertising and marketing, drug design and innovation, and product and process design and development. Indeed, the impact of gen AI on programming jobs is already being felt.

- Because AI models are extremely data hungry, they can be trained not just on the finished products, but also on data collected during the creation process. Any such data generated is typically owned by the organization, which makes it even easier to train future internal AI models.

- Most organizations are already sitting on large gold mines of past data, a lot of which can be successfully used to pretrain or fine-tune AI models.

Consider, for example, a team of engineers working on the drivetrain for a new model year of a car. Such a team may comprise several dozen individuals with a variety of skills and experiences. At the same time, all automakers have access to copious amounts of data from previous drivetrain creation including their performance, costs, and the design processes. It is therefore foreseeable that companies may look to shift more of the initial work to AI, thereby impacting several white-collar jobs in the area.

However, AI needs newer, cleaner, and larger datasets to learn from and improve its performance. Organizations relying on the current capabilities of the AI may sooner or later find out that the algorithms they use start performing worse than they used to through "model decay"—the degradation of the AI's performance over time. The reason is that the data with which they were trained is no longer representative of the reality in which the AI has to navigate.

Our preferences, context, and sense of humor, taste, and fashion change constantly. And we humans are needed to reveal our preferences, to laugh and engage when we find something humorous, and to wear a product that we find fashionable. The most precious data will be about us humans, and it is therefore our interaction with digital systems that results in that data. Eliminating the human implies eliminating the data about the person that the AI is designed to generate content for. Only we can determine whether we find *that* joke funny, whether that subtle change in color is fashionable, or whether something new is now needed, because just generating what we liked three months ago is not good enough anymore.

This very fact, which emerges only from the nature of AI and not from the nature of other technologies that have in the past affected the labor market, can surprisingly help align the needs of employers and employees, as human employees are fundamental for generating newer data that can eventually drive AI.

Data Cooperatives Are to Data what Labor Unions Are to Labor

In the context of work, it is the employees' on-the-ground knowledge, problem-solving abilities, and evolving skill sets that change with each new challenge and innovation. Thus, the most valuable data for the AI that can take over the tasks of the workers will come directly from the tasks workers perform, as their hands-on interaction with tools, systems, and customers generates the precise data that AI requires to stay accurate and useful.

It is here where data cooperatives offer a new approach to data governance by enabling workers to co-own and manage their collective data through a more or less decentralized decision-making process.[3] This happens because the members of a data cooperative can pull data currently siloed in different sources into one bundle. The aggregation of data that members generate from diverse sources and situations can lead to the development of new products, services, and business models that would be unattainable through individual contributions alone or through the utilization of data in single sources (like one company, one platform, one service provider, etc.).

Furthermore, once workers start seeing monetization of their data from cooperatives, they are much more likely to reorganize their own processes to facilitate better data collection, which in turn can generate better AI outcomes for the organization and higher incomes from data for workers.

Other than labor unions, which have traditionally sought a one-way route to improve the workers' conditions, data cooperatives operate like providers of training data and follow the rules of the market to satisfy an unsatisfied demand (the one of training AI systems with up-to-date data). And this can be made in privacy-preserving ways, such that the members of the cooperative keep their private insights private. This model of organization empowers workers by allowing them to establish shared rules for data use, potentially enhancing their bargaining power with employers. In practice, this requires that the data cooperatives enable workers to individually collect their data from different sources, deciding on a case-by-case setting which third party (like their employers, for example) can train an algorithm on that data. This enables workers to monetize their data and keep it controlled under one single umbrella. There are a number of models for how to do this: Some use blockchain, others use third-party apps, while others store data locally and simply give users more control over who has access to it and how it can be used.

Now that data is being increasingly used as a factor of production (i.e., as an input) in the economy, it seems natural that data cooperatives emerge as a solution. This is the same logic that led to development of labor unions in the past: The fragmentation of the ownership structure of the factor of production (be it data or labor) impedes any bargaining power of an individual with the employer.

Data and labor, both critical factors of production, do share the challenge of fragmentation. However, they differ in the fact that data mainly creates value in large volumes. Hence, its aggregation is required to unleash its value via insights. It is because of that required aggregation that we speak of "big data."

In the context of data cooperatives, the collective ownership model of data does more than just enhance bargaining power; it fosters the creation of value by leveraging the volume and diversity of its members' data. This illustrates how distributed ownership structures can drive broader economic and social benefits beyond mere negotiation leverage.

What This Means for the Future of Employee-Employer Relationships

For this economic value to be unleashed—and for both employers and employees to thrive in the data economy—everyone involved needs to raise their level of data literacy. Both workers and employers should understand how data creates value, which is by being aggregated and analyzed in order to reveal insights and patterns that can improve decision-making and train AI models. Further, workers should understand how they contribute to creating and managing such data while they are working and use the collective influence that cooperatives grant them in order to have the right discussion about the future of work.

To take full advantage of the data people produce, while also ensuring workers have control over which data they offer and are fairly compensated for it, employers and employees should follow these steps in order to be able to shape the future of the digital economy, and thus the future of work:

1. Assess the organization's internal data resources and potential

Employers and employees should begin by conducting a thorough audit of the data that the organization already collects and generates, focusing on identifying data that could be valuable for AI training or analytics. In that exercise, identifying the employee-generated data can serve as a basis to quantify the contribution of the employees to the data-based value generated by the organization. The "Workers' Algorithm Observatory" is an initiative born at Princeton University that enables workers to crowdsource data and investigate the algorithmic systems behind the platforms that determine pay, schedule, and more in the platform economy and beyond. Employers and employees can use this initiative for inspiration and support.

2. Engage employees in data literacy programs

Organizations can implement training programs to enhance their employees' data literacy. By educating them on how their daily activities generate valuable data, the importance of this data in AI development, and how they can participate in data cooperatives, valuable knowledge is created. This knowledge enables employees to generate more value by means of the organizations' data and, at the same time, enables all of the relevant stakeholders in the organization to have a common understanding and language about the value that data cooperatives can create. This benefits everyone: Employees better understand how they create value and are compensated for it, and employers get higher-quality data in return. The pharmaceutical company Roche is pioneering this area.

3. Incorporate data cooperative clauses in employment contracts

By updating employment contracts to include clauses that recognize employees' rights to their data and outline how their data can be used in cooperation with data cooperatives, organizations can position themselves as pioneers in this area. This would ensure transparency and provide a legal framework for data usage and can help with the attraction of new talent. These types of clauses are being discussed in initiatives like the Data Workers Union, which advocates for workers' rights over the data they generate. Companies can take inspiration from these discussions to craft their own policies and stay ahead of what promises to become a major labor issue, thus leading and shaping the discussion about this topic. By being proactive now, companies can develop a mutually beneficial system and head off a point of contention later on, at which point they might have to sacrifice more.

Given the dynamic nature of society, AI will (at least in the foreseeable future) need the data and guidance of humans to generate real value. Therefore, workers will play a fundamental role in keeping the AI relevant. It is the combination of labor, capital, and AI that will—if anything—generate the value that's being projected by consultancies such as McKinsey.[4] Workers should therefore focus on understanding the interplay between capital, labor, and data and start guiding the discussion about the future of work with the right understanding of the nature of the AI.

Business leaders should equally understand the dependencies between capital, labor, and data in order to proactively propose collaborative frameworks that let organizations—and thus society—flourish in the age of AI.

TAKEAWAYS

As AI continues to transform industries, tensions between employers and white-collar workers are rising. Workers are increasingly pushing back against AI's impact, with data ownership and usage becoming central to labor negotiations. Data cooperatives offer a promising solution by allowing workers to control, monetize, and leverage their data for better bargaining power.

✓ **Data ownership is critical, and AI needs fresh data.** Without continuous human input, AI models degrade, making worker-generated data indispensable. Workers generate valuable data, yet organizations typically own and use it without compensation.

✓ **The role of data cooperatives.** These cooperatives can empower workers to control and monetize their data, much like labor unions have in the past.

✓ **Employer-employee collaboration.** Companies should improve data transparency, implement data literacy programs, and integrate data rights into employment contracts.

✓ **A new labor paradigm.** Aligning AI, labor, and capital can create sustainable value for businesses and workers alike.

NOTES

1. Mary Towers, "The AI Bill Project," Trades Union Congress, April 18, 2024, https://www.tuc.org.uk/research-analysis/reports /ai-bill-project.

2. Daron Acemoglu and Pascual Restrepo, "The Race between Man and Machine: Implications of Technology for Growth, Factor Shares, and Employment," *American Economic Review* 2018, no. 108 (6): 1488–1542, https://ide.mit.edu/sites/default/files/publi cations/aer.20160696.pdf.

3. Stig Nyman et al., "From Algorithmic Management to Data-Driven Labour Organising," *Scandinavian Journal of Information Systems* 36, no. 1 (July 2024): article 2, https://aisel.aisnet.org/cgi /viewcontent.cgi?article=2040&context=sjis.

4. "The State of AI: How Organizations Are Rewiring to Capture Value," survey, McKinsey & Company, March 12, 2025, https:// www.mckinsey.com/capabilities/quantumblack/our-insights /the-state-of-ai.

Adapted from "Data Collectives Are the Next Frontier of Labor Relations" on HBR. org, September 27, 2024 (reprint #H08DSH).

7

WHAT DEEPSEEK SIGNALS ABOUT WHERE AI IS HEADED

by Toby E. Stuart

D eepSeek's launch of its R1 model in late January 2025 triggered a sharp decline in market valuations across the AI value chain, from model developers to infrastructure providers. Investors saw R1, a powerful yet inexpensive challenger to established U.S. AI models, as a threat to the sky-high growth projections that had justified outsized valuations. For those who have been paying attention, however, the arrival of DeepSeek—or something like it—was inevitable.

Even so, this is a useful moment to reflect on where AI is headed. Rather than understanding DeepSeek's R1 as a watershed, it's more useful to see it as a sign of where we really are right now—and a harbinger of what's to come.

Here are five lessons that business leaders should take away from this moment.

From Pattern Recognition to Problem-Solving

Large language models stole the show in 2023 and 2024, but in 2025 we will stand in awe of AI systems that can reason, plan, and operate autonomously. That's because two related trends will dominate the AI landscape this year: the rise of reasoning models and the arrival of AI agents that are ready for prime time. These capabilities heavily rely on reinforcement learning (RL), which is a method of training an intelligent agent to make a sequence of good decisions. Think of it like learning to play a video game. When you hit a bull's-eye or jump over a wide ditch or guess a word, you earn points. As you play, you learn to perform actions that are rewarded.

The last generation of models like GPT-4 were amazing pattern matchers—they pretrained on vast quantities of information, contextualized it all, and blew us away with their uncanny next-word predictions to respond to our prompts.

DeepSeek R1 is a free-to-all reasoning model—as are OpenAI's just-released ChatGPT o3-mini and Microsoft's Copilot o1 models. These models represent a crucial shift from uncertain next-word prediction to methodical problem-solving that heavily relies on RL. Reasoning allows them to perform certain tasks much better than prior models, like solving math problems. Think about trying to multiply two large numbers. Most people can't look at them and guess the answer—they need to pull out pencil and pad, break the problem into steps, and work it through. Reasoning models can increasingly do this, too.

With the capability to break down and reason through problems, AI agents are able learn to dynamically navigate complex workflows, adapting to new information as it arises in the process of task completion, rather than being limited to rigid, predefined scripts. This is just what humans do in our work, such as when customer service agents respond to queries, when admin employees create schedules and plan travel, and when data analysts collect information, analyze it, and write a report.

AI's Economic Inflection Point

One of the big headlines around DeepSeek R1 is its reported development cost of $5.5 million.[1] That figure is misleading. It likely only reflects the cost of a single training run, excluding infrastructure, engineering, and deployment expenses. A total figure that included those expenses would be much higher—though still significantly lower than the estimates of the development costs for OpenAI, Anthropic, Google, and other models R1 is competing against.

Instead of focusing on these numbers alone, we should be paying more attention to inference costs—the expenses associated with actually using models after they've been trained. Training requires substantial upfront investment, but inference costs are crucial for enterprise applications. DeepSeek R1 and other recent entrants, including Meta's Llama series of models, represent large reductions in these expenses. As a rule, falling prices tend to spur competition and drive user adoption. Just think about the drop in performance-adjusted prices in markets for all electronic products—smartphones, television sets, laptops—driven by efficiency gains in semiconductor production. This is Moore's Law propelling price drops and higher adoption rates of far too many end products to name. The same is happening in AI.

Open-Source and Proprietary AI Will Coexist

One reason we should have expected a development like DeepSeek R1 is the basic economics of open-source software. Historically, open-source projects have challenged proprietary solutions by significantly reducing costs, such as Unix/Linux in enterprise computing, Android in mobile OS, MySQL in databases, and, of course, Llama in AI. The cost advantage of open-source software is well documented. It is predictable that AI would follow a similar trajectory.

In AI, proprietary models from companies like OpenAI, Alphabet, and Anthropic remain at the cutting edge in multimodal capabilities, security (it appears to be easy to jailbreak DeepSeek R1), and other benchmarks. Even so, open-weight models like DeepSeek R1 have closed the gap in text-based reasoning, and the model is incredibly efficient. The potential for enterprise use cases of the model is reflected in Microsoft's overnight decision to integrate DeepSeek R1 into Azure. Because of their lower costs and greater flexibility, open models like DeepSeek

R1 will be very attractive to users. So will a host of small language models, like Microsoft's Phi-4, which have demonstrated strong performance in many use cases.

For now, it looks like we can expect a market structure with a diverse array of players, versus a winner-take-almost-all scenario.

Silicon Scarcity Drives Algorithmic Innovation

Another part of the reaction to DeepSeek R1 has centered on the "surprising" news that China appears to have closed the gap with the United States in frontier AI models. U.S. export restrictions were meant to limit Chinese access to the most advanced semiconductors and help preserve American companies' lead in AI research. (Some argue this only reinforces the need for such controls.) The fact that this approach hasn't completely succeeded should not be a great surprise. Remember the old adage, necessity is the mother of invention? The silicon constraints have led Chinese researchers to prioritize algorithmic efficiency over raw compute power—a strategy that could prove prescient as data center energy consumption explodes. But this fact—and the elegance of the algorithmic research done in China—has been true for some time. China's LLM landscape has been rapidly growing, with 117 LLMs available for public use last year. Despite strict constraints on training data and outputs, quite a few Chinese LLMs are competitive on global leaderboards, particularly excelling in Chinese-language tasks. The AI talent pool there is exceptional; DeepSeek itself has an extremely innovative research team, and the depth of AI talent in the nation is vast.

DeepSeek R1 Didn't Change Everything

All of this said, the major AI labs and the hyperscalers in the West—including Microsoft, Meta, Alphabet, and Amazon—will continue to invest at dizzying levels, ensuring that demand for state-of-the-art GPUs and AI infrastructure will remain high. Open models will not completely replace proprietary ones, and we are likely to see immense computational resources consumed in model training and inference. As a result, the neck-and-neck sprint for the most capable AI systems will continue to fuel demand for high-performance chips and large-scale cloud infrastructure, despite investment costs now vastly outstripping revenues for many players in the industry.

In addition, the big infrastructure buyers in the West are undoubtedly concerned about supply risk, since the majority of advanced semiconductors are manufactured in a TSMC facility located in Taiwan. Given the tension in U.S.-China relations and Taiwan's strategic value, major buyers in the West are likely thinking about stockpiling compute power.

The pace of AI advancement—as well as the social and economic importance of this set of technologies—arguably has no historical precedent. With reinforcement learning enabling breakthroughs in reasoning models and AI agents, which will in turn lead to countless new applications, the near future will be packed with "DeepSeek" moments. Expect continuous advancement, increasing real-world use cases, and the true beginning of a seismic-scale reshaping of the economy.

TAKEAWAYS

The launch of DeepSeek R1 signaled a shift toward reasoning-based models and AI agents capable of problem-solving. While it highlights China's AI advancements, it also reinforces trends in cost reduction, open-source adoption, and ongoing competition between proprietary and open AI models.

✓ **From pattern recognition to problem-solving.** DeepSeek's model demonstrated that AI is evolving beyond language models to reasoning and autonomous decision-making.

✓ **AI's falling costs.** Lower inference costs are driving AI adoption, much like faster processing speeds have shaped consumer electronics for decades.

✓ **Open-source versus proprietary models.** As an open-source model, DeepSeek R1 challenges proprietary systems by lowering costs, though proprietary models still lead in multimodal capabilities and security.

✓ **China's algorithmic innovation.** U.S. semiconductor restrictions have pushed China to optimize AI efficiency, leading to competitive advancements.

✓ **AI's unstoppable growth.** Despite shifts in competition, major AI companies will continue investing in large-scale infrastructure, ensuring rapid AI development and economic transformation.

NOTES

1. DeepSeek-AI, "DeepSeek-V3 Technical Report," https://arxiv.org/pdf/2412.19437.

Adapted from HBR.org, February 4, 2025 (reprint #H08MD2).

8

HOW COMPANIES CAN MITIGATE AI'S GROWING ENVIRONMENTAL FOOTPRINT

by Christina Shim

B y 2026, computing power dedicated to training AI is expected to increase tenfold over 2024 levels.[1] As more power is expended, more resources are needed. As a result, we've seen exponential increases in energy and, perhaps more unexpectedly, water consumption. Some estimates even show running a large AI model generates more emissions over its lifetime than the average car. A recent report from Goldman Sachs found that by 2030, there will be a 160% increase in demand for power propelled by AI applications.[2]

We know there is palpable environmental risk to operating this way indefinitely, but we also know AI can be a powerful new tool for sustainability, accelerating how quickly we solve problems, helping us understand and cope with climate change, and supporting the nascent energy transition.

AI adoption is the new normal for businesses and governments seeking to enhance decision-making, increase business productivity, and lower costs. That's why we need to consider more sustainable AI practices now, while also prioritizing AI use cases to power overall sustainability gains.

How can we effectively use AI and reap its benefits while minimizing environmental impact to the best of our collective ability?

Make Smart Choices About AI Models

An AI model has three phases—training, tuning, and inferencing—and there are opportunities to be more sustainable at every phase. At the start of an AI journey, business leaders should consider choosing a foundation model rather than creating and training code from scratch. Compared to creating a new model, foundation models can be custom tuned for specific purposes in a fraction of the time, with a fraction of the data, and for a fraction of the energy costs. This effectively "amortizes" upfront training costs over a long lifetime of different uses.

It's also important to choose the right size foundation model. Most models have different options, with 3 billion, 8 billion, 20 billion, or more parameters. Bigger is not always better. A small model trained on high-quality, curated data can be more energy efficient and achieve the same results or better depending on your needs. IBM research has found that some models trained on specific and relevant data can perform on par with ones that are three to five times larger, but faster and with less energy consumption.[3] The good news for businesses is that likely means lower costs and better outcomes too.

Locate Your Processing Thoughtfully

Often, a hybrid cloud approach can help companies lower energy use by giving them flexibility about where processing takes place. With a hybrid approach, computing may happen in the cloud at data centers nearest the needs.

Other times, for security, regulatory, or other purposes, computing may happen "on prem"—in physical servers owned by a company.

A hybrid approach can support sustainability in two ways. First, it can help you colocate your data next to your processing, which can minimize how far the data must travel and add up to real energy savings over time. Second, this can let you choose processing locations with access to renewable power. For example, two data centers may offer similar performance for your needs, but one draws on hydropower and the other on coal.

Lastly, it's important to only use the processing you need. Many organizations over-provision how much compute power is standing ready for their needs when software already exists to do better. In one case of our own AI workloads, IBM was able to reduce the excess, standby "headroom" from the equivalent of 23 to 13 graphics processing units (GPUs), significantly lowering energy usage and freeing up high-demand GPUs for other purposes—with zero reduction in performance.

Use the Right Infrastructure

Once you've chosen an AI model, about 90% of its life will be spent in inferencing mode, where data is run through it to make a prediction or solve a task. Naturally, the majority of a model's carbon footprint occurs here also, so organizations must invest time and capital in making data processing as sustainable as possible.

AI runs most efficiently on processors that support very specific types of math. It is well known that AI runs better on GPUs than central processing units (CPUs), but neither were originally designed for AI. Increasingly, we are seeing new processor prototypes, which are designed from scratch to run and train deep learning models faster and more efficiently. In some cases, these chips have been shown to be 14 times more energy efficient.

Energy-efficient processing is the absolute most important step to take, because it reduces the need for water-based cooling and even for additional renewable power, which often incurs its own forms of environmental costs.

Go Open Source

Being open means more eyes on the code, more minds on the problems, and more hands on the solutions. That level of transparent collaboration can have a huge impact. For example, the open-source Kepler project—free and available to all—helps developers estimate the energy consumption of their code as they build it, allowing them to build code that achieves their goals without ignoring the energy trade-offs that will impact long-term costs and emissions.

Open source also means tapping the "wisdom of crowds" to make existing AI models better instead of tapping our energy grids to forever build new models. These models will let resource-limited organizations pursue cost-effective innovation and reassure skeptical organizations with flexibility, safety, and trustworthiness.

The largest open-source project in history—the internet—was originally used to share academic papers. Now, it underpins much our economy and society.

Similarly, as we envision how AI may help bring about a better future, we must strive for innovation while simultaneously being mindful and responsible about the options we have and the natural resources involved.

TAKEAWAYS

As AI adoption accelerates, its energy and resource demands are increasing at an alarming rate. By 2030, AI-related power consumption is expected to rise by 160%.

To balance AI's benefits with its ecological impact, companies must adopt smarter, more sustainable AI practices.

- ✓ **Choose efficient AI models.** Use foundation models rather than training from scratch; smaller, high-quality models can reduce energy costs.

- ✓ **Optimize processing locations.** A hybrid cloud approach minimizes data travel and leverages renewable energy sources.

- ✓ **Use energy-efficient infrastructure.** Specialized processors can reduce energy use by up to 14 times compared to traditional CPUs and GPUs.

- ✓ **Embrace open source.** Shared AI models and energy-conscious coding practices improve efficiency and reduce redundant computing.

- ✓ **Plan for long-term sustainability.** Strategic choices in AI development today can significantly cut environmental impact over time.

NOTES

1. "Electricity 2024: Analysis and Forecast to 2026," International Energy Agency, January 2024, https://iea.blob.core.windows.net /assets/6b2fd954-2017-408e-bf08-952fdd62118a/Electricity2024 -Analysisandforecastto2026.pdf.

2. "GS SUSTAIN: Generational Growth—AI/Data Centers' Global Power Surge and the Sustainability Impact," Goldman Sachs Research, April 30, 2024, https://www.goldmansachs.com /intelligence/pages/ai-data-centers-global-power-surge-and -sustainability-impact.html.

3. "Enterprise Generative AI Made Simple: IBM's Differentiated Approach to Delivering Enterprise Grade Foundation Models," IBM.com, April 2, 2024, https://www.ibm.com/blog /announcement/enterprise-generative-ai-made-simple/.

Adapted from HBR.org, July 4, 2024.

PREDICTING AND BUILDING YOUR COMPANY'S FUTURE

9

MAKE BETTER STRATEGIC DECISIONS AROUND SLOW-DEVELOPING TECHNOLOGY

by Tucker J. Marion, David Deeds, and John H. Friar

S elf-driving automobiles may seem like a cutting-edge 21st-century technology—a challenge still facing obstacles before widespread adoption. But in fact, autonomous driving has been evolving in fits and starts for a full century. Its evolution can teach managers how to deal with innovations that depend on multiple slow-developing technologies that come together at different speeds and costs.

In 1925, Ford Motor Company exhibited a vehicle called the American Wonder that drove up Broadway and down Fifth Avenue—reportedly even navigating a traffic jam—without anyone in the driver's seat. Instead, the car was operated remotely by radio signals coming from another vehicle that was following behind it. It wasn't exactly "self-driving," but it was still a remarkable achievement for that era.

In 1958, General Motors exhibited an experimental prototype called the Firebird III, which featured an electric guidance system that allowed it to navigate an automatic highway while the driver relaxed without hands on the wheel. However, it worked only on a quarter-mile stretch of road with embedded circuits.

By 2005, five DARPA-sponsored autonomous vehicles successfully drove through a 150-mile-long course in the Mojave Desert. Since then, companies including Google, Tesla, Apple, and a host of startups have invested billions in autonomous driving technology—but despite the substantial investment, it's still being used only on a small scale in pilot projects in a handful of cities.

Why is making this technology commercially viable proving so challenging?

A self-driving vehicle relies on a range of technologies, including LiDAR sensors, MEMS sensors (such as accelerometers), GPS, 5G cellular communications, and artificial intelligence. These technologies have matured at different rates, and their cost trajectories have likewise evolved at different paces.

Consider, for instance, a LiDAR system, which shines lasers on a vehicle's surroundings and the objects in its path, measures the reflections, and uses the differences in return times and wavelengths to make digital 3D representations that determine locations. Hughes Aircraft Company introduced this technology back in 1961, and the National Center for Atmospheric Research was one of the first to use the technology to analyze clouds and air pollution. Initially costing millions, LiDAR systems now cost $100 to $200. Similarly, GPS capabilities, first developed during the 1980s, didn't become widely available until the early 2000s; by the mid-2010s, they became a chip-based technology that costs under $5 per unit. In the fast-moving field of artificial intelligence, the capabilities that allow autonomous vehicles to recognize obstacles and make decisions are evolving in capabilities and cost by the month. Only when the full suite of technologies is robust and affordable enough can autonomous driving fully deliver on the promise that researchers have contemplated for more than 100 years.

So how do companies manage when an imagined product relies on a group of innovations that emerge slowly—a concept we've come to think of as "slow-cooking technologies"? In these situations, when the development of the underlying technologies rises and falls over decades, tracking it and creating an R&D strategy around it (without investing too much too early) can pose a significant challenge.

Most corporations can't afford to invest much effort in tracking technologies that may take decades to be effective and affordable enough to commercialize. At the same time, when the right group of technologies reaches the right maturity and cost, they can be extremely disruptive—and because they often blindside companies, their impact can be devastating.

One example of that has been playing out in front of us: the internet. The academic version went online in 1969, but it took more than two decades (and the invention of internet protocols, HTML, the web browser, and eventually, broadband access) to power the dot-com boom and countless innovations in the decades since. It's an innovation that's disrupted entire industries, and companies that struggled to figure out the right time to invest in an internet strategy often didn't survive.

Determining when to place bets on emergent technologies is a science, not an art. The most fundamental thing a CEO should do is stop thinking about innovation through singular technologies. Although many executives don't realize it, the innovations that create new industries and ecosystems—or shake up existing ones—are often made up of multiple technologies. Instead, they should identify the various sciences and technologies that underlie a potential innovation and establish a process for monitoring and managing them as they develop—even if that may take decades.

Many companies neglect this because of a simple but incorrect belief: Waiting makes sense. The prevailing wisdom is that the greatest number of business opportunities will emerge after the technologies have been commercialized but before a competitor has time to dominate the market. Based on our research and professional experience, we believe this is a mistake. Companies that try this typically miss the opportunity and will never be in a position to gain an advantage.

Rethinking Technology Mapping

Companies already use sophisticated tools to predict how quickly a technology might be ready for commercialization. One example is the NASA-created Technology Readiness Level (TRL); another is diffusion curves. These visual representations are supposed to help with long-term R&D planning, research funding, and M&A strategy. Too often, however, these tools focus on forecasting individual technologies rather than the suite of innovations necessary to make something like autonomous driving possible.

In addition, companies have relied on futurists, expert panels, and trend extrapolation to assist in technology planning. However, these methods can be marred by personal fixations, opinions, and flaws in gauging market readiness. Above all, conventional technology forecasting doesn't work well when companies must cope with novel technologies and their interplay.

Take, for instance, some of the key technologies in the iPhone. Each developed along a different trajectory, became available at an extremely high price, and was first used in applications at the bleeding edge of technology. Lithium-ion batteries, graphical user interfaces, and densely packed silicon integrated circuits were pioneered in the 1960s. By the end of the decade, NASA had become the biggest buyer of integrated circuits, which fueled the growth of companies such as Fairchild Semiconductor and, later, Intel. The resulting fall in the price of eight-bit microprocessors led to the development of the first PCs, such as the Apple II, launched in 1977. Indeed, many of the technologies that make up an iPhone had been around for 50 years before the capabilities, sizes, and costs fell sufficiently for Apple to combine them and launch the iPhone in 2007.

The most effective way of coming to grips with transformational innovations is to identify all the emergent technologies that could affect an industry in the long run, prioritize them in terms of their possible functions and impact, and focus on the three or four key ones. That will require tracking research trends in universities and think tanks; analyzing government policy trends, venture capital, global foundations, and competitions; corporate R&D spending; and tracking NIH, NSF, and DARPA calls for proposals and outcomes. For instance, DARPA was highly active in autonomous vehicle activities in the early 2000s, and commercial automakers were paying close attention to vision systems, LiDAR, embedded machine learning, and early AI software.

Designing the Technology Feasibility Matrix

After identifying the most promising emergent technologies, companies must ask two questions about each: Can it work? And at what cost? The answers will allow you to create a Technology Feasibility Matrix, a two-by-two we find helpful in our teaching and consulting work.

FIGURE 9-1

The Technology Feasibility Matrix

As technology improves and costs fall, innovations will move toward mass market viability in the lower-right quadrant. For innovations that involve multiple technical advances, identifying where each technology is today and its likely trajectory toward the mass market can help companies develop the right strategy.

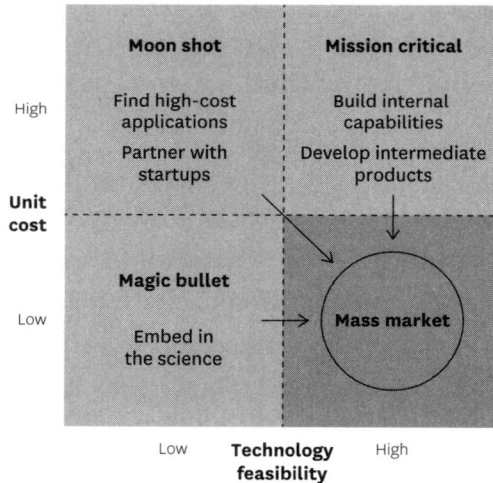

Source: Tucker J. Marion, David Deeds, and John H. Friar.

Technologies fall into four quadrants: moon shots, mission critical, magic bullets, or mass market.

The challenge of managing transformational innovations gets compounded when the underlying technologies fall into different quadrants at a point in time. In the case of autonomous automobiles, for instance, developing the artificial intelligence that can drive a vehicle is still a moon shot, while 5G cellular car-to-car communications are feasible but investment intensive because of the infrastructure that has to be created, making it mission critical.

That leads us to the next dimension of the problem: When will the underlying technologies of a transformational innovation likely come together? Although finding answers to that question may not be easy, it isn't impossible either. The key, our studies show, is to focus on cost.

By analyzing the R&D investments necessary to develop them and the production costs of the key technologies and projecting their future trajectories as far out as possible, it's possible to come to grips with how cost will influence the creation of a transformational innovation. That will allow CEOs to determine which technologies to work with and how to manage them, yielding a strategic focus for R&D.

It always takes a long while before the costs of all the underlying technologies fall to the point where companies can integrate them into a transformational innovation that can be manufactured at a viable price point. This represents a *cost convergence window*—the point at which it becomes possible for businesses to combine these technologies into new products within the foreseeable future. The ability to manage the convergence can make or break a company, so it's essential to get this right.

Consider Eastman Kodak, which could neither take advantage of its invention of digital photography nor its belated push into digital cameras and net-based print platforms. It had to declare bankruptcy in 2012, when social media and smartphones had changed entirely how users share and consume images. Kodak shows how navigating the convergence window is critical for incumbents—both early and late in the game—especially since challengers will be quick to use emerging technologies during this period. Startups tend to move quickly, creating winner-take-all network effects before all the technologies that can create a game-changing product or service emerge.

Companies can use several approaches to manage emergent technologies before commercializing:

- If they spot the convergence window early, there will be enough time for them to pursue a proactive approach. Proactive strategies allow companies to shape the trajectories of developing technologies so the latter meet their future needs.

- Another strategy is using intermediate products to build assets and refine capabilities. Netflix followed this strategy for 10 years by developing its DVD delivery business while broadband internet matured to the point where streaming became viable.

- Conversely, corporations that latch onto the convergence window later than rivals must move quickly to catch up with a reactive strategy. When the window narrows, companies can quickly pilot projects with advanced competitors, as Honda recently did with GM with its Prologue EV. This helps companies test applications and capabilities without over-committing resources while the market matures. In reactive efforts, companies can gain firsthand access to disruptive technologies by partnering with startups. We see this with dramatic growth in the number of pilots pursued between established corporations and AI ventures.

- Another option is targeting high-cost entry points, such as luxury or niche markets, which can sustain early adoption until costs fall further, as seen with luxury EVs or the use of integrated circuits in space and military applications in the 1960s and early 1970s.

Revisiting Technology Management Strategies

Although it's important to understand the disruptive potential of any new technology, the convergence of slowly evolving technologies is a more pressing challenge today. Managing it undoubtedly requires a meta strategy.

For one thing, CEOs shouldn't behave as if only the R&D or IT function needs to worry about the challenge; they must equip all levels of the organization to develop an understanding of emerging technologies. This aids road mapping, R&D, and planning for transformational innovations. The process will require the creation of multiple modes of inquiry and development, from building better innovation ecosystems to observing the technology culture of the next generation.

Teams that understand, develop, and implement these plans must span organizational boundaries. DARPA, for instance, has well-honed processes to bring experts from industry, government, and academia to work on specific projects with its teams. Cross-pollination increases knowledge quality, allowing technology teams and functions to develop a more complete picture of the future.

No organization can hope to develop a complete picture of all the technologies that may affect it or be able to predict every unexpected scientific discovery. But every organization can try to futurecast, which develops an understanding of tomorrow's possibilities and works back from it to create useful lines of inquiry. For instance, NASA's Convergent Aeronautics Solutions (CAS) Project is working with design firms, academic institutions, companies, startups, venture capitalists, and others to understand how air taxi technologies are evolving, a process it calls mapping. It is systematizing the mapping process to better understand and tackle gaps in current and near-future capabilities.

. . .

Over the last decade, businesses have started combining the engineering machinery, transportation systems, and physical networks spawned by the Industrial Revolutions of the eighteenth century with the smart devices, intelligent networks, and expert systems enabled by the Internet Revolution of the twentieth century to spark a fourth wave of global innovation. Consequently, nothing gives a company a competitive edge over rivals as much as disruptive technology does.

However, instead of simply waiting and worrying about getting disrupted, companies, especially the market leaders, would do well to manage the dynamics in what is proving to be a golden era of technological change and convergence. That requires investing time and attention into tracking slow-cooking technologies.

TAKEAWAYS

Technological breakthroughs often rely on multiple innovations maturing at different rates. Companies must navigate these "slow-cooking technologies" wisely to avoid missing opportunities or overinvesting too early. Autonomous vehicles and past innovations, such as the internet, illustrate how timing and cost convergence are crucial to success.

✓ **Beyond singular innovations.** Leaders should track entire ecosystems of emerging technologies rather than focusing on single breakthroughs.

✓ **Strategic timing matters.** Waiting until technologies are commercialized often results in missed opportunities. Companies must monitor cost and feasibility to act at the right moment.

✓ **Managing the convergence window.** Firms should adopt proactive, reactive, or hybrid strategies to integrate emerging technologies before competitors dominate.

✓ **Cross-disciplinary approach.** Collaboration between industries, academia, and government accelerates technological readiness and competitive advantage.

Adapted from HBR.org, January 14, 2025 (reprint #H08KQV).

10

WHAT 570 EXPERTS PREDICT THE FUTURE OF WORK WILL LOOK LIKE

by Nicky Dries, Joost Luyckx, and Philip Rogiers

"Technology has given us the moon landing, the personal computer, and the smartphone—not to mention indoor plumbing and washing machines," an optimist might say. "Why would we ever want to stop progress? We should be accelerating, not halting and regulating. AI and robotics are going to bring us into the post-scarcity age, making us all richer and doing our dirty work for us."

"Let's not get ahead of ourselves," a skeptic replies. "Newspapers have claimed that robots are coming to take over our jobs for 50 years now—it hasn't happened before, and it won't now. New technologies like AI will, however, increase productivity and efficiency, which leads to economic growth and to new and better jobs for people."

A pessimist retorts: "Not so fast. This time it really *is* different. Let's not forget that previous industrial revolutions indeed brought technological progress, but also had dramatic effects on the working and living conditions of workers of that time, which lasted for decades on end. There is no reason to believe that big business won't see automation as an opportunity to reduce labor costs, thanks to a workforce of robots and algorithms that can work day and night without ever needing a break, complaining, or getting sick. What we need is not more economic growth, but degrowth."

Who's right here: the optimist, the skeptic, or the pessimist? And which scenario do *you* personally believe in more?

Sorting Out Beliefs About the Future of Work

These two questions were the focus of our recent study.[1] To answer them, we first identified a set of 485 Belgian newspaper articles from the last five years, in which global experts made predictions about the future of work. Based on this newspaper analysis, we found that three specific groups clearly dominate the debate around the future of work in the media: tech entrepreneurs (like Elon Musk), economics professors (like David Autor from MIT), and bestselling authors and leading journalists (like David Frayne and his book *The Refusal of Work*). We found high agreement between experts from the same group about how they believed the future of work will play out and low agreement between the groups. (To our surprise, policy-makers, politicians, union representatives, and HR managers were largely absent in these articles.)

We then identified 570 experts from tech, economics, and writing/journalism, from both our personal networks and from larger mailing lists for Belgian CEOs and journalists. Our team wrote scenarios about the future of work (similar to the ones in our introduction but with more detail) based on the competing predictions made in the media and asked them to rate the likelihood of different predictions. All experts who completed the survey consistently believed that the scenarios pushed by "their" group in the media were more likely.

Next, we asked them to indicate, for each separate prediction, by what year they expected it to happen and with what degree of certainty. As expected, we found that

FIGURE 10-1

A timeline of future-of-work predictions

When asked to rank the likelihood of predictions made by tech entrepreneurs, economists, and journalists in 485 newspaper articles, 570 experts from these fields landed on the following course of events as most likely to occur.

- **2025:** Technology requires constant re/upskilling by workers.
- **2026:** Job tasks are partially automated.
- **2029:** New technologies create new types of occupations and industries.
- **2030:** More and more occupations are augmented by AI, helping people work more efficiently and productively.
- **2033:** Major ecological disasters occur.
- **2035:** Economic inequality increases dramatically.
- **2037:** People work alongside robot colleagues. More and more jobs are entirely replaced by technology.
- **2042:** Third world war breaks out.
- **2044:** Surveillance societies become the norm worldwide.
- **2046:** Automation leads to shorter workweeks, increased leisure time, and a renaissance of human craftwork.
- **2050:** Labor markets worldwide are faced with mass unemployment.
- **2051:** Governments introduce universal basic income.
- **2052:** Humanity depends on technology for everything.
- **2053:** Breakthroughs in longevity research drastically extend the lifespan of the technocratic elite.
- **2063:** Technocratic elites start colonizing other planets.
- **2065:** All human qualities are surpassed by intelligent technology.
- **2074:** Human civilization is irreversibly changed by an uncontrollable superintelligence beyond our comprehension (technological singularity).

Source: Nicky Dries, Joost Luycks, and Philip Rogiers, "Imagining the (Distant) Future of Work," *Academy of Management Discoveries,* 2024.

optimists mostly expected positive breakthroughs in the near future; pessimists believed in negative outcomes and saw them as imminent; and skeptics were more likely to indicate for many predictions that they would never happen or only in the very distant future. Assuming that each of these groups of experts held a piece of the puzzle, we averaged out their predictions and mapped them onto one timeline to produce a rather haunting "consensus" view of what the future of work might look like (see figure 10-1).

Finally, we had the three groups of experts take a personality test, which included questions about their childhood and about their current values and beliefs. We found that the tech entrepreneurs were radical optimists, the economists believed in rationality above all, and the authors and journalists held attitudes indicative of misanthropy and a belief that much in society is decided by those in power behind closed doors. We found that not only did these different groups of experts have very distinct personality types, their personalities also translated into competing beliefs about the future of work.

Thus, the tech entrepreneurs were the optimists, the economists the skeptics, and the authors and journalists the pessimists in our data.

To complicate matters further, based on our newspaper analysis, we concluded that all three groups of experts were truly convinced that their predictions about the

future of work were right and that the others were wrong—
and even preposterous. Economists, for instance, tended
to refer to bestselling authors as "doomers" and tech entrepreneurs as "hypers." They particularly loathed the idea of
degrowth, which they likened to institutionalized poverty.
Authors and journalists, from their side, could not understand why the other groups of experts did not see that there
are (or should be) limits to economic growth, especially in
light of climate change and global inequality. Tech entrepreneurs considered themselves the only group qualified
to make statements about advanced technologies that no
one but them really understands, especially politicians; in
their eyes, these people were "dinosaurs."

Why There Are Differences in Beliefs About the Future of Work

In general, members of each expert group found it hard
to understand how it was possible for the others to have
such different beliefs about the future of work. After all,
their predictions were based on objective numbers,
figures, historical trends, and scientific research—how
could anyone argue with that? The answer, of course, is
that each of these experts were trained in a specific field,
with its own set of rules and assumptions about how the

world works. Further, they are also taught what counts as evidence within their discipline—consider how different that will look in computer science, economics, and political science, for instance. These experts interact mostly with people from the same or similar disciplines, attend workshops, and read reports that reinforce the so-called "field frames" they have been socialized into. This leads to homogeneity within disciplines and heterogeneity between disciplines. It also explains why these competing groups of experts find it so hard to understand each other's point of view.

In summarizing the findings of this study to others, we typically quip that "we can't predict the future of work, but we can predict your prediction." When we do keynotes about the study, the audience often starts laughing when they recognize the script from their own discipline almost verbatim. Sometimes, executives remark that "they are typical economists" or "they are on team degrowth." While this may seem like it separates people into distinct categories, we also find that it gets them to listen and talk to each other with a more open mind. We believe that this is crucially important, as many of the challenges humankind will likely face in the future of work—such as the potential emergence of hyperintelligent AI or robots with fine sensorimotor skills—will require interdisciplinary task forces and cooperation. As our study shows, experts from different disciplines typically have different views on future risks and opportunities—and we know from research that embracing uncertainty and competing scenarios is in fact essential to long-term strategic planning.

The Future Is What We Make It

The implications of our study are potentially controversial in the current "post-truth" climate—are we saying that there are no objective facts in life, that everything is subjective, and that expertise is a myth?[2] We wouldn't go that far. Rather, what we believe our study shows is that as the future is not yet set in stone, it is impossible to determine who is right about the future of work. Instead, the future will be whatever we make it. In our view, the scenarios pushed by optimists, skeptics, and pessimists are all theoretically possible. Questions like "Will AI destroy a lot of jobs?" are thus misguided—whether AI destroys a lot of jobs or not will depend on the decisions made by *people* in the coming years. The question is thus not, "What will the future of work be like?" but rather, "What do we *want* the future to be like?" This reframes the future-of-work question as an arena for values, politics, ideology, and imagination, instead of a set of trends that can objectively be predicted. It also makes clear that the debate around the future of work is likely to get even more polarized in the years to come. One person's utopia is another's dystopia.

So, what can *you* start doing today? First, from now on, whenever you hear or read something about the future of work, don't just look at what is predicted (and by when), but also *who* is saying it and *why*. What vested interests do they have? What society do they want, and how does it benefit them? Second, what is *your* utopia for the future, and what is your *dystopia*? What should we do—or stop doing—in the short-, mid-, and long-term to move toward your desirable scenarios and to reduce the risk of undesirable ones? What can we do to avoid points of no return for the distant future, for instance, when we are thinking about the climate or superintelligent AI? And third, what do you have most control over from your position of power and influence in society? What forms of power and influence do you *not* have? Can you partner with others who have sources of influence complementary to yours and who share the same vision of utopia?

Based on our research, we would like to invite every citizen, every policymaker, and every manager and CEO to enter the public debate around the future of work to ensure that it unfolds within a social and democratic dialogue. The future is what we make it.

TAKEAWAYS

The future of work remains uncertain, shaped by differing perspectives from experts in technology, economics, and journalism. A study analyzing predictions from 570 experts in three groups—entrepreneurs, economists, and journalists—revealed that each group sees the future through the lens of their own discipline, leading to contrasting views that are difficult to parse.

- ✓ **Diverging perspectives.** Tech entrepreneurs are optimistic, economists are skeptical, and journalists lean pessimistic about automation and AI's impact.

- ✓ **Expert bias.** Each group believes their own predictions are most likely, shaped by their field's assumptions and evidence.

- ✓ **Uncertain future.** The study suggests the future is not predetermined but depends on societal choices and values.

- ✓ **A call to action.** Individuals and policymakers should actively shape the future by engaging in democratic discourse and strategic decision-making.

NOTES

1. Nicky Dries, Joost Luyckx, and Philip Rogiers, "Imagining the (Distant) Future of Work: Predictions about the Future of Work Depend on Who's Making Them," *Academy of Management Discoveries* 10, no. 3 (September 2024), https://journals.aom.org /doi/abs/10.5465/amd.2022.0130.

2. Mark B. Brown, review of Gil Eyal, *The Crisis of Expertise* (Cambridge, UK: Polity Press, 2019), in *Minerva* 58, no. 4 (September 2020): 657–660, https://www.ncbi.nlm.nih.gov/pmc/articles/PMC 7479293/.

Adapted from HBR.org, September 16, 2024 (reprint #H08E7E).

About the Contributors

SCOTT D. ANTHONY is a clinical professor at Dartmouth College's Tuck School of Business and the author of *Epic Disruptions* (Harvard Business Review Press, 2025).

DAVID DEEDS is the Schulze Professor of Entrepreneurship at the University of St. Thomas and academic director of the Schulze School of Entrepreneurship. He is also a cofounder of the Entrepreneurship and Innovation Exchange and FamilyBusiness.org.

NICKY DRIES is a full professor of organizational behavior at KU Leuven and at BI Norwegian Business School. Her research focuses on re-politicizing the future of work and stimulating democratic debate, using methods aimed at triggering people's imagination about the future like media analysis, robotic art and design, virtual reality, and science fiction movies.

JOHN H. FRIAR is an executive professor of management and entrepreneurship at Northeastern University.

JOHN GLASER is an executive in residence at Harvard Medical School. He previously served as the CIO of Partners Health-care (now Mass General Brigham), a senior vice president at Cerner, and the CEO of Siemens Health Services. He is cochair of the HL7 Advisory Council and a board member of the National Committee for Quality Assurance.

ROBBIE HUGHES led the clinical automation company Lumeon from its founding in 2005 through its acquisition by Health Catalyst in 2024. He has worked to redesign and automate mission-critical care processes for some of the leading health care providers across the globe, including Optum and Kaiser Permanente in the United States and Nuffield Health and Bupa in the United Kingdom.

AMIT JOSHI is a professor of AI, analytics, and marketing strategy at IMD, and specializes in helping organizations use artificial intelligence and develop their big data, analytics, and AI capabilities. An award-winning professor and researcher, he has extensive experience of AI and analytics-driven transformations in industries such as banking, fintech, retail, services, automotive, telecoms, and pharma.

JORDAN T. LEVINE is an entrepreneur and lecturer at MIT's Sloan School of Management, where he helps graduate students create new possibilities at the intersection of business and technology. He is also the founder of a blockchain-based environmental monitoring startup.

JOOST LUYCKX is an associate professor of business and society at IESEG School of Management and a research fellow at KU Leuven. His research focuses on legitimacy struggles over multinational companies in the global public debate, more desirable futures of work, alternative organizations, and neutralization of social movement activism.

TUCKER J. MARION is an associate professor of entrepreneurship and innovation at Northeastern's D'Amore-McKim School of Business and the Mechanical and Industrial Engineering Department, College of Engineering.

J. MARC OVERHAGE, MD, is the chief health informatics lead at Elevance Health. Previously, he was the director of medical informatics and a research scientist at the Regenstrief Institute and the Regenstrief Professor of Medicine at the Indiana University School of Medicine.

JOSÉ PARRA-MOYANO is a professor of digital strategy at the International Institute for Management Development (IMD Business School) in Switzerland. His research focuses on the management and economics of data and privacy, with a special focus on how organizations can use data analysis techniques and AI to increase their competitiveness. He is an award-winning teacher whose research has been published in top-tier academic journals.

MARK PURDY is a cofounder and director of Beacon Thought Leadership, an independent advisory firm focused on content development and training services.

PHILIP ROGIERS is an assistant professor of organizational behavior and organizational theory at University Ramon Llull, Esade Business School. His research focuses on the transformation and deconstruction of jobs, along with the exploration of alternative organizational forms that support a more human-centered future of work.

CHRISTINA SHIM is the chief sustainability officer at IBM.

TOBY E. STUART is the Helzel Chair in Entrepreneurship, Strategy, and Innovation; faculty director of the Berkeley Haas Entrepreneurship Program; associate dean for external affairs; and faculty director of the Institute for Business Innovation at the Haas School of Business, UC Berkeley.

AMY WEBB is a quantitative futurist, CEO of the Future Today Institute, and professor of strategic foresight at NYU Stern School of Business. She is the author of *The Signals Are Talking, The Big Nine,* and *The Genesis Machine.*

RAPHAEL YAHALOM is a cybersecurity expert, an affiliated researcher at MIT Sloan School of Management, and a cyber risk strategic adviser.

SCOTT ZOLDI is the chief analytics officer of FICO. He has received U.S. Patent 11574234 on the commercial application of blockchain to AI model development management. He is additionally the author of more than 130 software patent applications, with nearly 100 granted.

Index

Work is hard. Let us help.

Engage with HBR content the way you want,
on any device.

Whether you run an organization, a team, or you're trying to change
the trajectory of your own career, let *Harvard Business Review* be
your guide. Level up your leadership skills by subscribing to HBR.

HBR is more than just a magazine—it's access to a world of
business insights through articles, videos, audio content, charts,
ebooks, case studies, and more.

HARVARD
BUSINESS
REVIEW

SUBSCRIBE TODAY
hbr.org/subscriptions